TERENCE CONRAN
BATHROOMS
SIMPLY ADD WATER

conran OCTOPUS

First published in 2004 by
Conran Octopus Limited
a part of the Octopus Publishing Group
a Hachette Livre UK Company
2–4 Heron Quays, London E14 4JP
www.octopusbooks.co.uk
This paperback edition published in 2008

Distributed in the United States and
Canada by Sterling Publishing Co. Inc.,
387 Park Avenue South,
New York, NY 10016-8810

The right of Terence Conran to be
identified as the Author of this Work
has been asserted by him in accordance
with the Copyright, Designs and Patents
Act 1988.

British Library Cataloguing-in-Publication
Data. A catalogue record for this book
is available from the British Library.

ISBN 9781840915075

Consultant Editor Elizabeth Wilhide
Publishing Director Lorraine Dickey
Executive Editor Zia Mattocks
Editor Siobhan O'Connor
Art Director Chi Lam
Art Editor Megan Smith
Picture Research Manager Liz Boyd
Location Research Anne-Marie Hoines
Illustrator Russell Bell
Production Manager Angela Couchman

CONTENTS

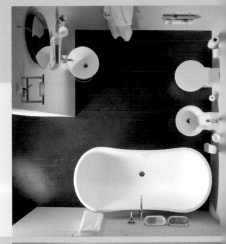

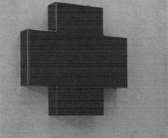

'Privacy and running water are a beautiful combination. Call them the two essential ingredients for clear thought.' AKIKO BUSCH, *Geography of Home*

The cultural history of bathing reveals that the practice of getting wet has often had little to do with getting clean. Even today, when the inexorable rise in water consumption in the affluent societies of the West might seem to indicate an almost neurotic anxiety about personal hygiene, other factors are plainly at play. Why do we bathe? We bathe, shower and otherwise wash for a whole range of reasons: for relaxation, for invigoration, for pleasure, for comfort, for hygiene, of course, and, perhaps, simply out of an instinct to immerse ourselves in an elemental, natural state, where we are once again cocooned, floating and weightless, in water.

Bathing has had a chequered history. At certain times, it has been a central social activity, at others an exclusively private one; in some periods, it has been widespread, in others rare. Throughout the ages, bathing has alternately been viewed as important for health and physical well-being and castigated as sinful indulgence. At the same time, bathing is not necessarily synonymous with water. Water may be the most common medium, but baths of mud, hot, dry air, or steam have often served the same purpose.

INTRODUCTION

ABOVE In Japan, bathing rituals are an important part of the culture. Cleansing is done prior to a long, contemplative soak in hot water. There are some 20,000 hot springs throughout the country, and spa resorts keep the tradition of communal bathing alive. Simplicity is an essential part of the experience, promoting an enhanced appreciation of nature. In recent years, the Japanese hot tub has become something of a status symbol in the West.

In very ancient times, washing was almost exclusively associated with purification rites. This ceremonial or ritual function remains a central part of many religions today. As part of their religious observance, for example, Hindus wash three times a day; in Islam, the ritual washing of hands, mouth, and nose is performed before prayer. These rituals have obvious counterparts in the Christian rites of baptism and the custom of making the sign of the cross after dipping fingers in holy water, and in the Jewish practice of washing hands before breaking bread on the Sabbath.

In parts of the world or at times when water was a scarce and precious resource, vital for crop irrigation, the body was cleansed by other means: ancient Egyptian nobility enjoyed asses' milk baths or skin scrubs with alkaline powders such as soda ash. Perfume was the sweetener for bodies imperfectly freshened.

The palace at Knossos, Crete, built by King Minos four thousand years ago, provides one of the first known examples of advanced bathing and sanitary facilities. The palace complex included baths, sinks, and cisterns, fed by a system of terracotta piping, along with the first-ever water closet, flushed from a reservoir and furnished with a wooden seat. Despite this level of development, bathing was not otherwise a feature of the domestic life of the ancient Greeks. In Sparta, for example, bathing was instead part of the rigorous fitness cult of that militaristic city-state. Following athletic competitions, bathing took place in public baths – a hot steam bath to produce sweat, followed by a plunge into a cold pool.

Steam bathing spread from ancient Greece both north and west, most notably to Rome, where bathing was to reach an unprecedented height of sophistication. The first Roman public steam baths date from the second century BC. At some later point, following the development of the hypocaust, a hot-air central heating system, Roman bathing embraced not only steam baths and plunge pools, but also baths of hot, dry air. Steam baths were necessarily one temperature, but the hypocaust system meant that rooms could be heated

to different temperatures, so bathers could progress from warm to very hot conditions. Roman bathing preserved the emphasis on physical fitness of the ancient Greeks, coupled with a new social, pleasurable role. Although there were private baths and washing facilities in the homes of the rich, most bathing took place in the great public baths, which, at their most developed, were virtual leisure centres, comprising libraries, shops, gardens, exercise areas, changing rooms, rest rooms, heated swimming pools, and other recreational facilities. The largest could accommodate thousands of bathers. Some had separate facilities for men and women; some were mixed. From archaeological evidence, it has been speculated that sexual services were among those recreations on offer in certain public baths – the Stabian baths at Pompeii were conveniently sited next door to a brothel.

Bathing for the Romans was an afternoon pursuit. Bathers rubbed themselves in oil and proceeded to the warm room, then to the hottest room, the *laconicum*, a steam room, before making their way to the *balneum*, the hot bath. Here, dirt would be scraped from the skin with a tool called a *strigilis*, and the bathers would immerse themselves first in warm water, then in the freezing plunge pool of the *frigidarium*. The process was often repeated, with bathers moving back and forth between steam and dry heat, warm and cold baths.

Sanitary facilities in ancient Roman times were equally advanced. There were nearly 150 public latrines in third-century Rome, and waste water from bathhouses was used to flush the communal latrines in Roman barracks.

The sophistication of Roman baths was founded on technical ingenuity. Aqueducts were used to transport water long distances, and examples of Roman lead piping have been discovered still in working order. With the spread of the Roman Empire, the Roman practice of bathing was exported all over the world – or at least all over the world that the Romans inhabited. In Britain, for example, there are more than 30 excavated sites, the most extensive of which is at Bath (Aquae Sulis), where the Roman baths are warmed by a hot spring.

ABOVE One of the most famous of all Roman spas is located at Bath, known in the days of the Roman Empire as Aquae Sulis. Taking the waters at Bath was a popular pursuit in Georgian times, and bathing in the hot springs continued until 20 years ago. Thermae Bath Spa, designed by Nicholas Grimshaw and Partners, is a new spa complex set to revive the tradition. Sited 100m (110yd) from the old Roman baths, the spa includes massage rooms, steam rooms, a solarium, and a rooftop pool of naturally heated mineral water.

RIGHT Until well into the twentieth century, bathing was a rudimentary affair in many parts of the world. A tin tub, filled by a 'copper' or by cans of hot water heated on the range, was the standard arrangement in many households. In those days, people generally bathed no more frequently than once a week. Not until a ready supply of hot water on tap became available did bathing become more about relaxing and less about getting clean for the majority of people.

After the sack of Rome in AD 476, the Roman baths in the western regions of the former Empire gradually fell into disuse. In the east, however, the bathing tradition survived in what became the Byzantine Empire, the capital of which, Constantinople (now Istanbul), had a complex water supply system. When this empire succumbed, in turn, to Ottoman invaders, the religious bathing practices of Islam were wedded to the Roman. 'Turkish' baths, or *hamaams*, were luxurious affairs, richly decorated in mosaic, with the same combination of steam rooms, warm rooms, and hot, dry rooms as the Roman model, but excluding the cold plunge pool. Massage and other forms of relaxation and refreshment were on offer: the emphasis was decidedly recreational.

By and large, feudal Europe enjoyed no such amenities. The Romans' knowledge of plumbing and central heating was lost and forgotten, except in the monasteries, where both bathing and sanitary arrangements were considerably better than the norm. Otherwise, hygiene was primitive to say the least. During the Dark Ages, not even monarchs bathed more frequently than once every three weeks, and it must be assumed that the large proportion of the peasant population went their entire lives unwashed. In ordinary households, bathing was a similarly rare albeit communal affair, with family members making simultaneous use of the same large, wooden tub, laboriously filled with buckets of heated water. A certain amount of refinement was, however, displayed at table. Courtly behaviour dictated the ceremonial washing of face, hands, and teeth at mealtimes – a necessary gentility in an age when forks were unknown and food was eaten with the fingers.

The typical medieval arrangement for sewage disposal was a far cry from the flushing water closet of Crete's King Minos. In castles, the 'garderobe' was a stone or wooden seat set over a shaft built into the wall, which discharged waste into the castle moat or into a pit. In towns, privy closets were either built over pits (which required emptying by 'nightmen') or discharged directly into rivers or streams, an arrangement which inevitably contributed to the spread of the plague, not to mention other diseases.

When Crusaders brought home news of Eastern bathing habits, for a short period during the fifteenth century Turkish baths were common in Western cities such as London and Paris. These 'stews' or 'bordellos', however, soon degenerated into establishments that were no more about bathing than today's backstreet 'saunas' and 'massage parlours' are about sweating it out in a pine cabin. Accordingly, the Church clamped down on the public baths and they were closed. The primitive nature of bathing in medieval Europe was not entirely a product of lack of technical expertise – it also reflected a profound suspicion of any practice that smacked of hedonism or personal vanity. Care of the body was irrelevant, prideful, and frankly heretical when care of the soul was all that mattered.

Although the accoutrements which accompanied bodily functions – the chamber pots and close stools, bidets, basins, ewers and baths – became increasingly decorative and ornamental from the Renaissance onwards, personal hygiene and washing habits were not much improved over the next few centuries. The first design for a flushing water closet

RIGHT Packwood House, a Tudor mansion built towards the end of the sixteenth century, was comprehensively restored and remodelled during the early decades of the twentieth. The bathroom is tiled with 407 whole eighteenth-century Delft tiles and 63 part tiles. A lion's head spout fills the bath.

was drawn up by a certain Sir John Harington during the reign of Elizabeth I and installed in his own house near Bath three hundred years before such fixtures began to appear in ordinary homes. Otherwise, it was business as usual: we owe the British colloquial term 'loo' to the warning *gardez-l'eau* that preceded the discharge of chamber-pot contents from upper windows into the street below. Chamber pots were kept in close stools, which were upholstered boxes with hinged lids and padded seats. No wonder people were anxious to take evasive action when they heard the dreaded shout.

Throughout the eighteenth century, various water-flushed devices gained in popularity among the upper classes; ball valves were introduced to flushing tanks and stink traps eliminated smells. The most successful system was designed in 1778 by a cabinet-maker, Joseph Bramah. Bramah's 'valve closet', still in production over a century later, consisted of a pottery bowl set within a panelled wooden casing and served by metal working parts. The eighteenth century also saw a new vogue for spa bathing at various European hot springs. Baths in wealthy households were draped and padded affairs, but generally the superficial appearance of cleanliness achieved with scent, face powder, coiffed wigs, and elaborate clothing masked the less salubrious reality of verminous, unwashed bodies.

Cleanliness did not become universally associated with godliness until the Victorian period, an era of technological innovation, mass manufacture, social upheaval, and outward moral crusade. In major urban centres, the impact of the Industrial Revolution brought matters of hygiene to a crisis point. The example of London provides a case in point. In the nineteenth century, London was the world's leading city and the hub of what was the greatest empire in history. In 1810, its population reached a million people, breaking the record previously held by Imperial Rome; by 1851, two and a half million people lived in the capital, the lower classes in conditions of unimaginable squalor. Indeed, until the 1850s, water was rationed in London, and soap itself was heavily taxed until 1853 – small wonder then that London's poor earned the tag the 'Great Unwashed'.

The 'Great Stink' of 1858, when the reeking open sewer that was the Thames forced the question of public sanitation under the noses of legislators, led to the building of London's impressive sewer network, designed by the great Victorian engineer Joseph Bazalgette. In 1854, Dr John Snow established the link between the cholera epidemics that plagued the summer months and contaminated water supply, although this was not widely accepted until a decade later. By the 1860s, however, the clean-up had begun. Piped water supplies were available all over the city, either in street standpipes or kitchens.

Such developments, along with falling soap prices and the provision of municipal baths, laundries, and washhouses, where an hour's bath could be had for a penny, began to see a gradual improvement in overall public hygiene. Public toilets were introduced in the late 1880s. By this time, cleanliness was firmly associated with both moral worth and social advancement: the first step on the rung to righteous respectability. In comfortable middle-class homes, armies of servants providing for the owners' every need made it easy to keep

ABOVE Memorabilia and whimsy have traditionally been a feature of bathroom decor, particularly in the smallest room. Family photographs line the walls of this bathroom in the home of Lucy Dahl, daughter of the late children's author Road Dahl.
LEFT A retro-style bathroom in a Belgian house has been decorated in moody shades of green. Pedestal sinks and claw-foot bathtubs are widely available from reclamation yards and similar sources.

ABOVE In warm, sunny climates, the act of open-air bathing has considerable appeal. Here, an aluminium tank sunk into rock is fed by a water pipe which has been routed underground.

clean and decent. Before hot water on tap, tubs were filled with cans of hot water which had been heated on the kitchen range; bedrooms had individual tiled washstands with porcelain basins and jugs for morning ablutions. In the public arena, Turkish or steam baths, sometimes known during this period as 'Russian' baths, made a reappearance, too.

A wide range of designs for water closets were patented and marketed in the second half of the nineteenth century by inventors and sanitaryware manufacturers who have since gone on to become household names. Twyford, for example, was one of the first to devise an all-pottery pedestal closet which required no casing. Shanks was another leading manufacturer, while Thomas Crapper is today chiefly remembered as the inspiration for a particularly ripe slang term. Many late Victorian WCs were highly decorative, with moulded detail and transfer patterns; high-level cisterns were the norm to provide a sufficient head of water pressure for the flush.

The urban and rural poor often had to make do with the most rudimentary facilities – tin washtubs or the public baths, outdoor privies. The middle and upper classes, however, enjoyed a considerable degree of comfort in the years that preceded World War I. Hot, running water was no longer a rarity, and Edwardian bathroom fixtures and fittings were impressive in both design and performance. With the advent of the cinema, bathroom design became a vehicle for luxury, glamour, and exoticism.

The development of the bathroom in the twentieth century is not, however, a story of unbridled technological improvement and increased domestic comfort. In parts of the world where a large proportion of the housing stock dates back a hundred years or more, bathrooms and toilets have tended to be slotted into existing layouts in an ad hoc fashion. As home owners have generally been reluctant to sacrifice what might otherwise serve as a bedroom, such facilities often occupy quite cramped, restricted spaces. Remnants of Victorian prudery and a certain coyness about bodily functions have also meant that until relatively recently the bathroom was a fairly clinical, if not punitive, place: easily cleaned, but perhaps not so easily enjoyed. While North American arrangements have always been both more generous and more efficient in terms of performance than those in Europe, the average mid century bathroom was still relatively compact and utilitarian.

In the past decade or so, all that has changed. Today, as the home assumes greater importance as a private refuge from the strains and stresses of everyday life, the bathroom is emerging as the refuge within the refuge, a place of retreat and restoration. Not only has the bathroom grown bigger – the average American bathroom, for example, is now three times the size it was – but we have more of them as well. The ratio of bathroom to bedroom in many American homes now approaches, and sometimes exceeds, one to one. Second or third bathrooms are no longer the rarity they once were in European households.

With this shift of gears has come a new breadth of choice, not merely in decorative finishes, but also in terms of fixtures and fittings. The contemporary interest in material quality has seen bathrooms and showers sleekly clad in a host of evocative surfaces, from

glass block to mosaic, travertine to terrazzo, rubber to steel. Standard fittings have been transformed into elemental sculptural forms – the sink reinvented as a glass bowl or stone trough, the tub refashioned in concrete, teak, steel, and glass. And, increasingly, the modern preoccupation with personal fitness and well-being has seen the introduction of features more commonly associated with health clubs and luxury spas: steam rooms, saunas, pulsating power showers, and even whirlpool baths where ultrasound enhances the massaging effect of water jets. Fully waterproofed wet rooms that return bathing to its most elemental, open-plan bedroom/bathrooms, and self-contained serviced pods provide further evidence of changing design approaches.

'Signature' bathrooms and toilets in public buildings such as restaurants, bars, and hotels have inspired many of these approaches. The pampered luxury of the traditional Ritz- or Savoy-style bathroom has given way to innovative and often surprising designs that push the boundaries of convention and expectation. I am reliably informed that the women's loo in the London restaurant Mash features an expanse of mirror into which is inset two tiny television screens filming the men's. For sheer irreverence, it is hard to beat the Starck-designed urinal in Felix, a Hong Kong nightclub, where you pee against a large

ABOVE A more sophisticated take on the open-air bathing experience is provided by this indoor/outdoor bathroom in a lodge at the edge of the Kruger National Park, South Africa.

plate-glass window that offers a view of the cityscape. I recall staying years ago in a hotel in Positano where the bathtub was sited so you looked out to the sea. A pane of glass was set into the wall at the end of the bath, with another sheet placed in front of it: between the two swam goldfish, merging with the watery view.

Unsurprisingly, given the sophistication and range of products on the market, the bathroom has become an area of considerable domestic expenditure, rivalling kitchens. At the upper end of the UK market, the average spend on a master bathroom is a staggering £30,000. Sanitaryware manufacturers are drafting in big-name designers to transform their ranges, and we are proud to have designed a range for Villeroy and Boch called Aveo; branded bathroom fittings and fixtures crop up in the sales literature of estate agents as lures for potential buyers.

Whatever your approach, taste, budget, or requirements, designing bathrooms throws up a number of unique challenges. As an essentially fitted area, the bathroom must accommodate a number of fixed elements in such a way as to make the best use of available space. Then there are the practical issues regarding servicing, waterproofing, heating, and lighting which require different solutions to those employed in other areas of the home.

Above all, however, as the place where we begin and end the day, and where we care for ourselves at the most fundamental level, the bathroom plays a key role in creating a sense of well-being. Crucially, that means it must appeal to the senses – sight, sound, smell, and touch. Nowadays, getting away from it all begins at home.

Whatever its size and whatever your budget, the bathroom requires thorough planning. To begin with, good planning will help you to make the most of the available space; if you don't have much room at your disposal, this side of things assumes even greater importance. At the same time, bathrooms are essentially fitted areas, even more fitted in many instances than kitchens, and mistakes are expensive and disruptive to remedy. You don't want to discover once bathroom fixtures are installed that you don't have sufficient elbow room at either side of the sink, or to find that getting in and out of the bathtub is unnecessarily awkward.

This section is devoted to the basics of planning and layout. In many cases, the parameters of what you can and cannot do will be dictated by existing servicing arrangements, so there is also information about plumbing: water supply and pressure, drainage, and waste disposal. Although fitting a new bathroom will inevitably entail assistance, at the very least from a plumber, gaining a working knowledge of servicing will enable you to brief professionals correctly and to formulate realistic plans.

PLANNING & LAYOUT

LEFT A sliding door partitions a shower area from the rest of the bathroom. There is a sink in each area. The warmth of the wood panelling throughout adds depth of character.
RIGHT Back-to-back layouts simplify servicing arrangements. Here, double sinks are plumbed on the other side of a partition wall from the bathtub.

ASSESSMENT

Good planning is founded on detailed assessment, of both existing conditions and your personal requirements. Creative daydreaming can open your mind to new possibilities, but it's not a bad idea to set a notional budget right at the outset. Nowadays, the sky's the limit when it comes to the cost of bathroom fixtures and finishes, and it's a good idea to keep your plans grounded in financial fact before your vision outstrips your bank account.

Your budget will dictate not only what you can afford in terms of choice of fitting or materials, but also the potential level of change. For example, if you have only a little to spend, it might be better to forget about replacing existing fixtures and instead make a decent job of redecorating and installing new surfaces and finishes, rather than revamp the entire bathroom in an essentially substandard way. At the same time, if you are already planning a major scheme,

such as building an extension or converting a loft, adding a new bathroom or shower to your plans can be much more cost-effective and far less disruptive than carrying out the same work at a later date. Bear in mind that, although basic redecoration may not require any additional help, anything more extensive will demand the services of a variety of qualified professionals, and you will need to factor fees for such work into your budget. Be realistic about what you can afford, but don't let it stymie your imagination.

People plan new bathrooms for all sorts of reasons: to upgrade old fittings and fixtures, to improve decoration and renew tired surfaces and finishes, to ease the strain on a bottlenecked main bathroom or to install features, such as showers or bidets, that were previously absent. A good starting point, therefore, is to identify all the functions that the new area must provide.

How many bathrooms do you need? In North America, it is far from uncommon for every bedroom to have its own bathroom, along with additional cloakroom facilities for guests. Elsewhere in the world, most households enjoy nothing like this ratio. An additional bathroom or cloakroom can vastly improve a family's daily routine and prevent an acrimonious start to the day.

If the bathroom is to be shared, who will be using it? Safety is always a prime concern, but children and the elderly or less able have specific requirements. Double sinks can ease the strain in family bathrooms. Wall-hung fixtures provide clear space underneath which allows for wheelchair access.

Aside from the basic bathtub, toilet, and sink, what other features do you want to install? Popular options include: showers, bidets, laundry appliances, exercise equipment, Jacuzzis, hot tubs, and whirlpool baths.

How much storage do you require? Small cloakrooms may need only to incorporate storage for essential toiletries and supplies; larger bathrooms can be fitted out to serve as towel and linen stores and dressing rooms. Many people like to keep medicines and cosmetics in the main bathroom – the accoutrements of personal care can devour storage space.

What type of mood are you trying to create? Do you want somewhere streamlined and efficient where you can get yourself ready for the day ahead with the minimum amount of time and trouble? Or do you want to create a bathroom that serves as a restorative home spa, somewhere to linger, relax and soak your cares away? Do you relish the elemental quality of a wet room or are you after a more furnished result?

How much privacy do you require? Some people are comfortable baring all, while others need a greater degree of seclusion. Your attitude and approach to privacy may have an impact on possible sites for bathrooms and showers, as well as on the detailing of partitions, screens, and windows.

Existing conditions will dictate how far these requirements can be met. If you are building from scratch, there will inevitably be far fewer restrictions in terms of siting, size, and structure. If you are rejigging layout or altering an existing bathroom, there are a number of factors to consider. The most obvious, of course, is the size of the space at your disposal and where the existing plumbing is located.

▶ If space is strictly limited, consider borrowing extra room from adjoining areas or annexing cupboard space. Moving a partition wall out a matter of a few centimetres can make all the difference between a cramped layout and one that is truly workable. Removing a wall between a bathroom and adjoining toilet can increase the options.

▶ Alternatively, think laterally. If you can't fit everything into one space, consider hiving off certain facilities, such as sinks or showers, into separate areas. For example, providing sinks in children's or teenagers' rooms can go a long way to easing the pressure on a family bathroom. A shower occupies less space than a tub.

▶ If your plans entail dramatically increasing the weight on an existing floor, because you are installing a heavier bathtub or using a heavy flooring material, you need to check with a surveyor that the floor structure can bear the additional load. If you are installing a bathroom or shower in an attic space, joists will almost certainly need to be strengthened, usually by doubling up.

▶ If you are contemplating wall-hung fixtures, check that the wall structure is strong enough to hold them. Stud or plasterboard partitions will be unable to bear the weight.

▶ If your home is located in an area where the water is hard, you may wish to consider installing a water softener, which

ABOVE Wall-hung fixtures, along with a vertically mounted heated towel rail, make the most of available space in a bathroom slotted in under the eaves. A pair of skylights set in the roof plane provides natural light. **RIGHT** In a type of island layout, a custom-built concrete 'table' houses an inset sink, with taps (faucets) mounted on a wood block. The same mix of materials is repeated in the bath surround for a unifying effect.

will prevent the build-up of limescale and other mineral deposits, and add to longevity of fixtures and fittings.

▶ Planning regulations in many parts of the world stipulate that a toilet must not open directly off an area where food is prepared or eaten. The minimum degree of separation required is a small, ventilated lobby, with a door at either end, one accessing the toilet and the other accessing the kitchen or dining area.

▶ Bathrooms can be fully internal, that is, they do not require windows. Adequate ventilation or mechanical extraction is, however, still necessary by law.

▶ Review existing heating and lighting arrangements. Is the bathroom heated sufficiently to be comfortable? Does the lighting create a pleasant atmosphere?

▶ Seek advice to help shape your plans. Depending on the scope of the work, you may need to consult an architect, surveyor, plumber, or electrician to identify potential structural or technical issues and to ensure that what you want to achieve is both feasible and legal.

ABOVE In-line layouts simplify servicing and make the best use of narrow areas. Here, sink and bathtub are aligned along the same wall within an integral structure that serves as both vanity unit and bath surround.

RIGHT A half-height partition separates a shower area from the rest of the bathroom. The taps (faucets) for the sink are mounted directly on to the partition, while the shower head is flush with the ceiling.

SITING A BATHROOM

'Top of the stairs, first on the right.' There is, unsurprisingly, a certain predictability about bathroom location. Unless you are building from scratch, existing plumbing arrangements will be the defining factor when it comes to deciding on possible locations for bathrooms and cloakrooms. In older, storied houses, servicing tends to be stacked in some form of vertical core. Siting a bathroom, cloakroom, or other type of washing facility in line with this core is therefore simpler, cheaper, and less disruptive. In apartments and single-storey dwellings, kitchen and bathroom or bathrooms are often back-to-back, so that pipe runs are similarly shared. Many unfitted loft shells and loft-style apartments come with a choice of servicing points, offering greater flexibility.

Plumbing considerations aside, other important issues include access and privacy. In terms of access, it makes sense to bracket bathrooms closely with bedrooms because both are primarily used at the beginning and end of the day. The perennial appeal of the 'en suite' arrangement is the seamless progression from waking to showering or bathing to sleeping within the same private, intimate space. Where other family members share the bathroom, a democratic location readily accessible by all is preferable. Easy access also dictates that in an ideal world there should be a toilet and sink on every floor of a storied house. Supplementary facilities such as these do not need to occupy much space and can be squeezed into otherwise redundant areas under the stairs and similar locations.

As homes are becoming more and more open plan, with a free flow of activities resulting in fewer partitions and conventional room layouts, walls are also beginning to come down round that formerly private sanctum, the bathroom. Bathtubs have yet to take centre stage in main living areas,

but the bathroom/bedroom has definitely arrived. A popular halfway point is the bedroom only minimally screened from a bathing area by means of a half-height or half-width partition, the partition often conveniently serving as a headboard.

Similarly, as we become less coy about bodily functions, bathrooms are increasingly sited where there is an easy connection with outdoor areas. Fresh air, sunshine, and garden views enhance the fundamental sense of well-being that bathing and showering promote. Strictly speaking, bathrooms don't need natural light or windows that open as long as there is good artificial light and efficient mechanical extraction, but a bathing area that keeps some contact with the outdoors is often much more pleasant and soothing.

We may be less puritanical than our ancestors – or even our parents – but most people still appreciate a degree of privacy when it comes to lavatorial matters. Surrealist film-maker Luis Buñuel's 1974 satire of manners, *The Phantom of Liberty*, featured a famous scene where dinner guests sat round a table, each openly defecating on his or her own toilet, only to retreat, singly, to a small private room to eat in furtive isolation. That reversal of public and private retains its power to shock today.

LEFT Bath and shower are housed in an extension with fully glazed roof, separated from the rest of the bathroom by a glass-block screen.
ABOVE A bathroom immediately adjoins a bedroom in a converted loft. Double sinks are sited within the sleeping area.

BEGINNER'S GUIDE TO PLUMBING

Putting in a new bathroom necessarily demands the services of a plumber; it may also require electrical work, carpentry and joinery, and design assistance. The simplest course of events is to opt for the type of package deal offered by mass retailers of bathroom fittings or the design and fitting service of a specialist outlet (see page 216). Otherwise, you will need to hire individually and manage all work yourself. In both cases, however, it is useful to understand the basics so you gain a full appreciation of the practical factors that may limit or shape your plans and can brief qualified professionals properly – in their own terminology, if possible.

Water supply

All plumbing systems consist of a network of pipes – supply pipes to bring water into the home and waste pipes to take it out of the home. Simple layouts are cheaper and less prone to breakdown, and this often means that servicing runs are grouped within a core or arranged vertically. There are two main types of system: indirect and direct. Leaving aside the complexities of heating systems, in the indirect supply of cold water, mains water – clean, cold, potable water – is delivered to the home via a rising main which feeds both the cold-water kitchen tap (faucet) and a storage cistern (usually located in the attic space of a storied house). Pipes from the storage cistern feed other cold-water taps, the hot-water cylinder (if any), the boiler (if any), and toilets. For this reason, strictly speaking the cold-water kitchen tap is the only supply of fresh drinking water and the only water under mains pressure. Unless the base of the storage cistern is at least 3m (10ft) above the shower head, there will generally be insufficient water pressure for showering without the installation of a pump.

The indirect system was devised before the turn of the twentieth century at a time when burst water mains

LEFT A Starck bathtub forms the centrepiece of this sleek, contemporary bathroom. The glazed door on the right of the picture leads to a shower. **ABOVE RIGHT** There are two principal types of plumbing system: the indirect and the direct. The former is most common in Britain. Clean water is routed to a storage cistern and subsequently fed to all cold taps (faucets) except the kitchen tap. In the direct system, used elsewhere in the world, mains pressure water is routed directly to all fixtures.

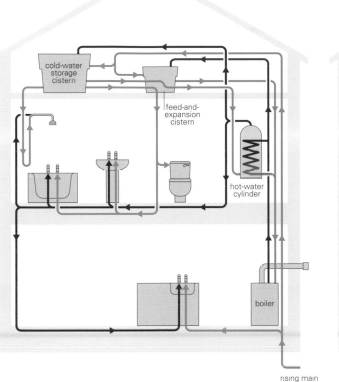

INDIRECT PLUMBING SYSTEM

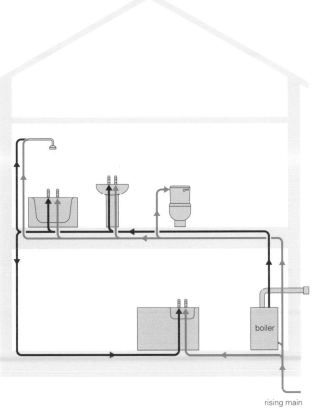

DIRECT PLUMBING SYSTEM

were a not infrequent occurrence. Legislation made it a requirement to have a storage cistern so that in the event of an interruption in the mains supply there would be a reserve of water in each household for basic needs. While this has been the norm in Britain, houses built in the past 40 years generally have a direct cold supply.

In the United States and continental Europe, on the other hand, the water system has always been direct. Cold, potable mains water enters the home under mains pressure and is routed directly to sinks, baths and toilets, as well as to washing machines, dishwashers, air-conditioning units, and heating systems. This means that all cold taps supply drinking water and that there is sufficient pressure for showering, wherever the shower is located.

These two systems have had a crucial effect on the design of bathroom fittings and fixtures. British taps, for example, are traditionally chunky affairs, with wide bores which are designed to deliver sufficient volume of water where there is not the benefit of high water pressure. European designs, by contrast, have developed along more minimal lines because water pressure is high. Similarly, the typical British shower head looks more like an overscaled rose on a watering can in comparison to the small, adjustable heads seen on European and American models.

Legislation regarding water supply has now changed in Britain, so it is now possible to have both a direct cold-water supply and a direct hot-water supply. This means that the more efficient European or American taps and shower heads will now work and showers do not require supplementary pumps. Additionally, combination boilers mean that there is no longer a need for a hot-water cylinder or cold-water storage cistern, which can have the benefit of freeing up additional space for bathroom use. Where a combination boiler must serve more than one bathroom or a power shower, however, it is necessary to have storage for hot water under pressure.

LEFT Jacuzzis, whirlpool baths, and other hydrotherapy fixtures impose their own requirements in terms of servicing. This sunken bath has controls mounted directly on the floor.

RIGHT Routing plumbing through partitions and similar features conceals it from view, but pipe runs must be accessible when problems arise. Here, necessary access is provided by a small panel at the partition's base.

FAR RIGHT Mechanical extraction of some kind for ventilation is a legal requirement where bathrooms are fully internal.

Drainage

There are two types of waste water: grey water, which is mildly soiled water from sinks, bathtubs, basins, bidets, and washing machines, and black water or sewage from toilets. All waste water drains either to the main sewer (usual in urban areas) or to a septic tank (more common in rural locations without access to servicing). Septic tanks need to be pumped out at regular intervals.

Drainage is aided by gravity, so all waste pipes must slope in a gentle gradient to keep drains running freely. The minimum recommended 'fall', or slope, is 6mm (¼in) for every 300mm (12in), and pipe runs should not exceed 3m (10ft). Siting sinks or other bathroom fixtures very far away from the main drainage stack tends to be ruled out by the difficulty of achieving the required gradient.

Waste pipes have U-bends at the point at which they drain from the fixture. This U-bend acts as a water trap which prevents smells rising from the drain. Waste pipes carrying grey water may connect before flowing into the main waste drain or vertical stack; toilet waste pipes, however, must connect directly to this soil pipe. The soil pipe is vented in order to equalize the pressure within the waste pipes, prevent air blockages, and propel sewage to the underground drain. The soil pipe must extend beyond windows and above roof level so that unhealthy vapours are dispersed. In older homes, there may be two separate waste pipes, with waste water from baths and sinks draining into a waste pipe feeding into a trapped gully at ground level, and waste from toilets draining into a soil pipe connected with the main drains.

Pipework

These days, most pipework is made of either copper or plastic. In the past, lead piping was more commonplace (the word 'plumber' derives from the Latin *plumbum*, meaning 'lead'), and some older properties may still have the odd bit of lead pipework, often in the form of a rising main. Old soil pipes tend to be cast-iron; new ones are plastic. Taps (faucets) and stopcocks are generally made of brass because this metal can be machined very precisely.

Copper piping is more expensive than plastic, but looks neater and is less noisy. Plastic piping tends to be used most

frequently for waste pipes. Depending on the type of plastic, however, it can be used for hot or cold water, does not burst when frozen, and does not corrode in the way that metal pipes do. Domestic plumbing systems often include both metal and plastic pipework. All metal pipework must be earthed; if a section of metal pipe is replaced with plastic, the bond to earth must be reinstated. Hot-water pipes must be insulated. In Britain, piping is now made in metric sizes, but bear in mind that existing installations may feature piping in old imperial measurements, which can cause difficulty when making connections.

Unless you intend to make a feature of it, visible pipework is generally an eyesore, and the art of plumbing is to design runs that are easy to conceal. If you are renovating an old property, running pipework on the surface is cheaper than gouging out channels in the walls and plastering over the top, but in the long run it may well be worth the extra effort and expense of choosing to do the latter. Neat, straight lines of pipework can also be boxed or painted in with the walls or skirting boards. Remember, surface-run pipework brings the risk of an accidental scald.

Troubleshooting

▸ Make sure that you know where stopcocks are located so the mains supply can be turned off in an emergency. There should be a stopcock inside your home and a water board stopcock outside between the water main and the rising main. Plumbers recommend that you turn a stopcock back half a turn from fully open to prevent it sticking.

▸ There should be access points at various locations to enable blockages to be cleared easily. Trouble is more likely to occur if pipework is overly complicated, with many branched connections or changes of direction.

▸ Pipework that is located under ground-level floors or in attics should be lagged and insulated to reduce the risk of burst pipes. Maintain a level of background heat if you leave your home unoccupied for long periods during the winter.

▸ If water begins to drain slowly from a sink, bathtub, or shower, use a proprietary chemical cleaner to dissolve the obstruction in the waste pipe before it builds up to form a total blockage. Hair and soap scum accumulate in waste pipes, but regular cleaning can keep things running smoothly so you don't end up with a plumbing emergency.

DESIGNING THE LAYOUT

Even if you intend to seek professional advice, whether it be from an architect, interior designer, or in-store design service, it is a good idea to draw up an initial floor plan yourself. This will give you some idea of how much you can fit into a particular area and will also serve as a briefing guide when it comes to seeking further assistance.

Provided you follow a few simple rules, drawing up an accurate scale plan is not difficult. The first step is to make a rough freehand sketch of the area in question, noting the position of existing features, such as windows, doors, and radiators. Take basic measurements and label the sketch. Make sure, however, that you choose one system of measurement and stick to it. Most bathroom fittings and fixtures are sold in metric sizes, so it makes sense to follow suit. Measurements must be accurate, not approximate; steel tape measures are best.

The second step is to transfer this information to graph paper using a steel rule and a sharp pencil. A scale of 1:20 is appropriate for bathrooms. Mark the features previously noted on the scale plan. Include the position of power points, light fixtures, boilers, and other fixtures. Don't forget to indicate which way the door opens. If you are updating an existing bathroom and intend to keep the servicing arrangements the way they are (by far the cheapest and least disruptive option), you should also indicate the position of sinks, tubs, toilets, and other fixtures. If you are creating

LEFT Scale plans and templates are invaluable when it comes to planning a new bathroom layout and deciding how much space you need between fixtures. Try out different permutations until you find the optimum solution. In a small or awkward space, options may be limited; larger areas offer more scope for different arrangements.
ABOVE RIGHT A circular wall partially encloses a shower area. Twin sinks encased in wood are wall-mounted. The black marble floor is a unifying element.
RIGHT A black wooden shelf and drawer unit extends to form the surround of the tub. This fitted 'island' is in keeping with the space's architectural character.

a new bathroom, one way of visualizing alternative layouts is to make templates of fixtures and storage units, and move them about on your scale plan. These should be drawn to the same scale, using the same system of measurement.

Height is another critical factor in bathroom planning, and you may also need to make a scale drawing of each wall (otherwise known as an elevation). Work to the same scale as the floor plan and note the ceiling height, the dimensions of windows, doors, and other openings, and the position of any fixed features such as boilers or radiators.

In 1974 Professor Alexander Kira of Cornell University published *The Bathroom*, the result of his studies into the ergonomics of bathroom use. As previous studies had done for the kitchen, in order to come up with recommended sizes and clearances, Kira's research looked at the way we move or position ourselves when using bathroom fixtures. For example, he noted that when a person stood at a sink, cupping their hands to raise water to their face, the arms made a triangular shape, down which water would run off. If a sink is not as wide as the distance between the elbows, water will therefore splash on the floor.

RIGHT There are three distinct zones in this modernist bathroom designed by British architect David Chipperfield. A partition separates the black basalt bath from the toilet cubicle, while the washing area is recessed into the wall and side-lit dramatically. Equally dramatic is the use of concealed lighting at floor level. The wall opposite the bathtub is infilled with glass windows from floor to ceiling, with the upper panes being openable.

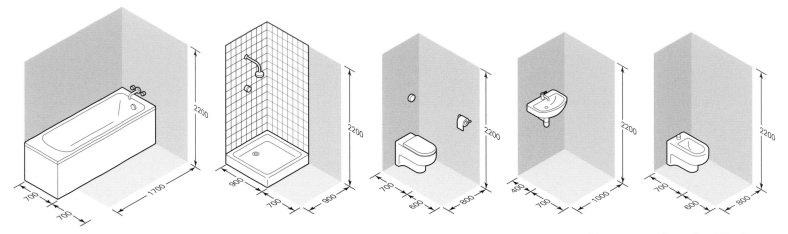

All measurements are in millimetres

Kitchen design is often underpinned by the concept of the 'working triangle'. Professor Kira's studies notwithstanding, there is no single formula applicable to bathroom layout. A further complication is that, while kitchen units are generally available in standardized rectangular modules, bathroom fixtures come in a range of different sizes and shapes, which adds an extra degree of difficulty to spatial planning. The placement of toilet, bathtub, shower, and sink is more to do with making sure there is sufficient room in front of or around each fixture for comfort and ease of use. A cardinal rule is either to provide some separation or to partition between the toilet and the rest of the bathroom – or at the very least to ensure that the toilet does not align with the head of the bathtub. Ideally, the toilet should also not be positioned so it is the first thing you see when you open the bathroom door. Sinks are best sited where there is good natural light for shaving and applying make-up.

All plans have to start somewhere. The position of the toilet can be a pivotal factor when determining the layout because there must always be an easy and straightforward connection between the toilet and the soil pipe. If the area is already plumbed, there may be very few choices about where the toilet can be sited. Alternatively, the bathtub, which occupies the greatest floor area, might equally serve as the starting point of the design. Plumbing runs are simplified significantly if bathtub and sinks, or sinks and toilets, are aligned along one wall.

Full head height is not necessary in all areas of the bathroom. Showers, of course, require standing room; baths, however, can be sited under sloping ceilings as long as there is adequate clearance for getting in and out of the tub. Similarly, toilets can also be positioned where the ceiling slopes, provided there is standing room in front.

Studying your scale plans might suggest ways in which you can improve function and proportion. High, narrow spaces often look better if you drop the ceiling or raise the floor; you might also consider the possibility of rehanging a door so it opens in the other direction or blocking in an existing window to provide room for a shower. (For further suggestions relating to design and layout, see Design Approaches, pages 40–131.)

Typical dimensions and clearances

▸ **Toilets** – standard depth 700mm (27½in), plus 600mm (24in) clearance in front.

▸ **Bidets** – standard depth 700mm (27½in), plus 600mm (24in) in front and space to either side for legs.

▸ **Bathtubs** – standard size 1700mm (67in) long x 700mm (27½in) wide; clearance of 700mm (27½in) alongside if the tub is sited lengthways.

▸ **Showers** – standard size 900mm (35½in) x 900mm (35½in), plus 700mm (27½in) clearance in front.

▸ **Sinks** – standard depth 400mm (15¾in), plus 700mm (27½in) clearance in front and at least 200mm (8in) to either side.

ABOVE LEFT The diagrams show typical dimensions of bathroom fixtures, along with minimum clearances for access and comfortable use. These days, however, bathroom fixtures come in many non-standard shapes and sizes; always check the dimensions of fixtures you intend to use with the supplier. **THIS PAGE** This bathroom, which was conceived as a series of 'rooms' off a connecting corridor, is principally finished in polished concrete that takes on a soft, smooth look in the diffused natural light from the window at the far end. The double sinks are set in a deep alcove above wooden drawers. On the opposite side, there are two distinct spaces, one of which houses a bathtub and the other a walk-in shower.

Today, the bathroom is no longer an afterthought, clinically fitted out and inhospitably decorated and detailed. It is a room in its own right, as much part of the home as bedrooms, kitchens or living areas. With this shift of attention and emphasis has come a much broader approach to design.

All bathrooms by definition are places where we go to get clean, but they serve many other purposes as well. For many of us, there's no better place to think: those 'Eureka!' moments occur with pleasing frequency in the bath or shower. Others cannot conceive of bathing without an accompanying book; some see the bathroom as the focus of a personal rite of well-being that takes in exercise as well as more passive therapeutic treatments.

This chapter examines common approaches to the contemporary bathroom, approaches that may be dictated by size or shape, or simply by lifestyle and preference. Although there is inevitably a degree of overlap – a family bathroom may be awkwardly shaped, a wet room may be small – these categories nevertheless provide the opportunity to address specific solutions and practicalities. Each section is illustrated by one or more case studies that illustrate in greater detail how different approaches work in practice.

DESIGN **APPROACHES**

LEFT A snaking curve of copper tubing serves as a heated towel rail on the wall behind a claw-footed bathtub.
RIGHT Muted lilac walls, white-painted floorboards, a stone fireplace, and a Venetian mirror provide an elegant setting.
BELOW A freestanding tub is positioned in front of a balcony to make the most of views and light. Bookshelves and retro furnishings promote an easy-going mood of relaxation.

BATHROOM LIVING

The bathroom as living area implies a generous, relaxed approach.
All bathrooms should be places where one welcomes spending time.

In the case of a 'living' bathroom, you may never want to leave. Absorbing the bathroom – or at least the bath – within another room is one way of emphasizing a more 'living' role. Another is to treat the bathroom as a living area of its very own, fitted and furnished to provide an extra dimension of comfort. Bathrooms with fireplaces, enough space for built-in clothes and linen storage, and furnished with sofas, chairs, and other pieces spell out the message that living does not stop short of the bathroom door.

Although they may not necessarily be as spacious, en suite bathrooms, or bathrooms directly adjoining bedrooms, also fall within this 'living' bathroom category by virtue of their interconnectedness. The most successful en suite arrangements are those where both rooms are considered as a whole in terms of design and decoration, underscoring the natural progression from one area to the next.

Siting

It is fair to say that 'living' bathrooms demand more space than average: creating that sense of generosity does tend to demand extra floor area. Many of the features and fixtures that contribute to this mood of relaxation are also in themselves not particularly compact. A fully inclusive 'living' bathroom needs space to accommodate one or more related functions. This could well be a dressing area, perhaps, or it may be somewhere comfortable to sit. Then there is the question of breathing room: an area where there is some free space around fixtures and fittings is much more relaxing than a tightly planned layout where you cannot help but be aware – however subconsciously – that absolutely every square centimetre is accounted for.

Whatever your stage in life, the 'living' bathroom places relaxation and personal care at the centre of the picture. Many couples treat themselves to this type of bathroom once children have grown and started to leave home, thus freeing a former bedroom for conversion, not to mention spare time for self-indulgence. On the other hand, the childfree and unattached might equally find the sacrifice of a second bedroom or living area well worth the sybaritic gain.

It is not always necessary, however, to borrow space from elsewhere in the home. If you have a large enough bedroom, you might consider siting the bathtub and other facilities within it rather than commandeering a second room.

In recent years, as walls have come down around conventionally designated rooms to create a free flow of multipurpose space, the bathroom has also been more closely integrated with other areas, most especially with the bedroom. The en suite arrangement, where the bathroom immediately adjoins the bedroom, is an obvious manifestation of the natural link between these two areas: both are private places that essentially frame the day. The closer they are, the easier the transition between waking and bathing, or bathing and sleeping. An en suite bathroom, accessible only through the bedroom, is a refuge within a refuge, and its exclusivity is undoubtedly part of the appeal.

Take the same idea a step further and you arrive at the open-plan bedroom/bathroom, where the bath is out on view. In older homes, bedrooms are often generous and well proportioned, which makes it easy to incorporate a bath without losing critical floor area. By the same token, a modern en suite bathroom may not be particularly large and removing

ABOVE A flexible variation on the en suite theme features a sliding door between the bathroom and the bedroom with its adjoining outdoor terrace. **FAR LEFT** Here, the dark tones of the chocolate-brown walls are picked up in the dark wood flooring of the bathroom and painted tub. **LEFT** A frosted-glass panel on runners connects a bedroom with a mosaic-tiled bathroom. A pivoting screen serves as an internal window.

the partition wall between it and the bedroom can enhance an overall feeling of spaciousness. If you are not quite ready for total exposure, removing the door between an en suite bathroom and bedroom gives the suggestion of connection, as well as improving natural light. Other halfway measures include partitioning the bathing area from the sleeping area with a glass screen (frosted or etched if privacy is an issue) or siting the bathroom behind a half-height or half-width partition that doubles up as an overscale headboard.

You will need professional guidance from an architect or structural engineer if such alterations entail structural work, such as removing all or a portion of a load-bearing wall. There may also be official permissions to negotiate with your local council or planning department. Good ventilation is essential, backed up by mechanical extract if necessary. You may welcome the liberating feeling of showering or bathing in the same room as the one in which you sleep, but not at the expense of sleeping in a humid, steamy atmosphere.

LEFT When space is generous, there is no need for strict coordination. Here, a pedestal sink with integral pearwood vanity unit, from Starck's Edition 1 range, has been combined with a period-style slipper bathtub on chrome feet.

RIGHT A sunken bath positioned at the end of a sunken bed built into a platform creates an intimate relaxation zone. The reflective pearly finish used on the walls, ceiling, and surround adds subtly to the sensual appeal of the room.

Design and layout

When you have plenty of floor area to play with, the possibilities for a more dynamic layout are increased. In a small space, you necessarily have to work hard to fit everything in, which tends to mean following the basic contours of the space. In a big room, fixtures do not need to be wall-hugging. Take advantage of this fact and consider siting a bathtub in a prominent position, either centrally, projecting at right angles from the wall, or perhaps in front of a bay window. Free space on either side of the tub – or, even better, all round it – adds considerably to the mood of relaxed contemplation. This can be further enhanced if you site the tub to take advantage of a view.

Another way of injecting a sense of drama while providing a sense of separation between different functions or activities is to position the tub at a different level, raised on a shallow platform, for example, or, conversely, sunk into the floor. Building a platform in order to sink a tub within it is generally the cheapest and easiest way of achieving this effect.

Modern shower fixtures, minimal and elegant, barely intrude. Spray and water splashes, unfortunately, do. A shower cubicle or circular shower enclosure is a good way both of incorporating this feature in an otherwise open-plan area and maintaining essential separation between wet and dry areas. The curvaceous form of a shower screen also adds a certain sculptural interest. If you have enough room, you can dispense with a shower screen altogether and simply waterproof the shower area; a gentle slope to a central drain set in the floor prevents water running off on to adjacent surfaces (see page 94 for the design of wet floors).

Even in a generously proportioned space, washbasins and sinks are often best aligned with a wall, to make service runs neater and to facilitate the building in of related storage facilities. In an open-plan bedroom/bathroom where you want only the bathtub on view, you might consider concealing sinks within a storage wall that can be closed off behind doors when not in use. The same solution can be adopted to provide privacy for the toilet where you are also sleeping in the same room; alternatively, a three-quarter partition could serve as the necessary screen.

Dressing areas integrated into 'living' bathrooms liberate space in bedrooms and sleeping areas. Le Corbusier regarded the traditional practice of keeping clothes in the bedroom as 'unhygienic'. One does not need to share his rather tetchy obsession with cleanliness to appreciate that a bedroom which is not dominated by storage is a more peaceful and restorative place, nor to acknowledge that bracketing dressing areas with bathing facilities makes good, practical sense. A wall of seamless cupboards, customized with shelving, hanging rails and cubbyholes, can house an entire wardrobe. In the case of adjoining bathrooms, dressing areas can be compactly planned in the form of vestibules that link sleeping with bathing areas.

ABOVE Claudio Silvestrin is one of the world's acknowledged masters of minimalism. In this Silvestrin-designed apartment in Milan, the spare, elemental quality of the architecture provides a serene contemplative atmosphere, where bathing and washing almost take on the significance of a ceremonial rite. When less is more, detail is all-important. Here, panels of thick glass serve as a screen between sleeping and bathing

areas, allowing natural light from the four floor-to-ceiling windows to reach the entire space. The shower is a simple curved pipe, with drainage arranged so that water flows away between the large stone slabs; the sink is a carved stone model mounted on a stone top; both are Silvestrin designs. Stone is a material with great presence and a certain monumental quality.

Surfaces and finishes

Many of the materials and finishes which are practical in bathing areas can be a little hard, cold and unrelenting for bedrooms. This is particularly true of flooring, necessarily experienced barefoot in both locations. One solution is to combine different materials in the same area – carpet or natural-fibre flooring in the sleeping part of the room, for example, tile, stone or mosaic in wet areas. This is more successful if there is a natural break between the two, such as a semipartition or change in level, and if both types of material share the same colour and tone. Where a break is more overt, as with adjoining bathrooms, it is still important to consider both rooms together when it comes to decorative choices. Matching tones or colours enhance a sense of connection and allow the two spaces to read comfortably as one, even where different materials are employed.

If you aren't someone who regularly soaks the floor or splashes about, wooden flooring, provided it is properly sealed, can serve throughout the space, perhaps accessorized with a rug at the bedside. In the same way, a rug adds a welcome touch of comfort to a large 'living' bathroom, and there will be enough floor area to ensure it is positioned away from showers and bathtubs. Another good unifying floor is poured rubber – soft and warm enough to suggest comfort, but waterproof, too. It can be slippery when wet, so provide a well-anchored mat beside the tub.

Stone or tile is not most people's first choice for an area which accommodates both bathing and sleeping, although, in a hot climate, the hardness of these materials is more than offset by the welcome feeling of coolness underfoot. In temperate parts of the world, underfloor heating will take the edge off the chilliness.

ABOVE French designer Andrée Putnam's open-plan bedroom/bathroom has a chic contemporary edge. An egg-shaped carved stone bathtub sits on a mosaic base inset into the hardwood floor. **ABOVE RIGHT** This large bathroom adjoining a master bedroom features double sinks, a freestanding claw-foot bathtub and generous wardrobe and linen storage. **RIGHT** Slatted teak flooring makes a surprisingly practical surface in a wet area. The concrete half-height partition screens the custom-made concrete sink from the bedroom.

ABOVE Before indoor plumbing, baths were taken in portable tubs brought to the bedroom and filled with hot water by hand. Something of the boudoir remains in this elegant bathroom, furnished with a delicate French wickerwork settee and featuring an original stone fireplace and parquet floor. The cast-iron bath, panelled screen, antique chandelier, ladderback chair and mirror reinforce the gentle period mood.

Furnishings and fixtures

A bathroom where the emphasis is on 'living', no less than one which is essentially open plan, demands fittings and fixtures that are worthy of scrutiny. In particular, the focus falls on the bathtub, especially if it is prominently situated. In this context, it is no use opting for the type of tub that is more usually built-in or aligned with a wall. It will simply appear stranded and out of place. Instead, here is the opportunity to display more sculptural designs in all their glory – from rolltop claw-foot period pieces to double-ended oval tubs or large round baths. Choosing a tub in an unusual material can also help to reinforce the 'living' mood, while, if you're a sociable bather, a large double-ended bathtub can accommodate two comfortably.

Similarly, vessel-type sinks in the form of bowls or troughs, or sinks inset into cabinets or tables, marry better with a furnished setting than standard bathroom ranges; existing pieces of furniture can be customized in this way if you are after a period look. Wood, terracotta, or stone sinks inject a note of tactility.

A chaise-longue, a sofa, or a chair or two accentuate the 'living' side of things, providing somewhere to pause and read the paper or curl up with a book, or simply offering a more comfortable perch for a pedicure than the side of the bath or the toilet seat. Other freestanding pieces of furniture, such as armoires and chests for linen storage, or a table for setting down books or drinks, pursue the same relaxed theme.

ABOVE A long, wooden refectory table set against the wall gives a furnished look to this country bathroom, with its rolltop tub and exposed floorboards.
LEFT The concrete bedstead and sunken tub are complemented by different flooring materials – wood around the perimeter of the bed, and stone elsewhere. Generous white drapes soften the look.

What you exclude is just as critical as what you include. It's important not to be too heavy handed with furnishing – clutter will rapidly undermine the sense of calm that spacious surroundings evoke. On a more practical note, you should also avoid swathing the room in fabric and other forms of soft furnishing. A 'living' bathroom may be furnished, but it is still a place that is subject to humidity. Expanses of carpet or heavy drapery will simply absorb warm, damp air and deteriorate quickly. And bathrooms that have grown up to become living areas aren't really the place for washing machines and clothes dryers.

Special features

'Living' bathrooms spell out the message that relaxation is just as important as the functional necessities of bathing and grooming. Features more typically associated with living areas, such as fireplaces and music systems, go a long way towards promoting this sense of enjoyment.

In fact, there can be very few pleasures that are more elemental than bathing in front of a roaring fire on a winter's day, the cosy focus of the flames providing a mesmerizing accompaniment to a long, soothing soak. Integrated music systems are another bonus for improving atmosphere, especially for those who regard showering or bathing as the perfect excuse for a little impromptu vocalization.

Although personally I relish the opportunity to escape the flicker of the television screen, for those addicts who cannot tear themselves away from the box there are now televisions which are designed especially for bathroom use, with heated demisting screens to prevent the build-up of condensation. These are normally available as built-in features, inset so that the screen is flush with tiling or panelling. One particular model suitable for the bathroom is only 12.5cm (5in) deep.

As with any living area, it is important to pay attention to the quality of artificial lighting. Dimmable lights allow you to vary the mood, depending on your inclination or the time of day. And, of course, bathing by candlelight has perennial appeal, particularly if the candles are scented.

ABOVE Essential viewing? There are now televisions designed especially for bathrooms, with heated screens to prevent condensation. Some models fit flush with the wall.

RIGHT A curved concrete partition separating a living area from a large slate-clad bathroom features a built-in fireplace that provides a cosy focus on either side of the divide.

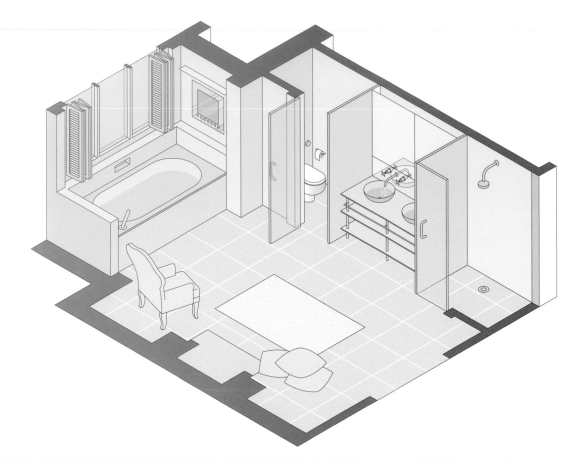

LEFT With bathroom features tucked neatly into alcoves, the rest of the room can be furnished as a living area with an armchair, rug, and floor cushions. The washing alcove, particularly, has been precisely planned and built. Working with toughened safety glass leaves no room for error.
BELOW LEFT The undermounted steel bathtub is enclosed in frosted glass. The splashback is limestone to match the floor. A television specially designed for bathroom use is inset in the wall at the foot of the bath.

CASE STUDY **BATHROOM LIVING**

A generous bathroom is supremely luxurious. Large spaces, however, need careful planning so that bathroom fixtures and fittings do not appear stranded. This master bedroom and bathroom suite on the first floor of a London townhouse has been designed so the bathroom amenities slot into alcoves around the perimeter, leaving the rest of the room to be furnished as an additional living area. With the bathing alcove aligned with the double doors leading to the bedroom and the basin alcove positioned opposite the fireplace, the basic layout has a symmetry in keeping with the original architecture.

Otherwise intrusive features, such as the shower and toilet, have been accommodated in glass cubicles to either side of the washing alcove. The tight planning, high specification of fixtures and fittings, and extensive use of glass called for an exceptional degree of precision, in both detailing and construction. Concealed in high-level cupboards above the washing alcove are all the servicing elements, including a high-level cistern, steam generator, extracts, air-conditioning units and fan-assisted heating.

ABOVE The cubicle to the right houses a power shower, with body jets and steam functions. A galvanized steel shower tray lies below limestone flooring. Both the toilet and shower cubicles are lined in limestone tiles. Sinks are glass bowls mounted on an open glass unit with towel storage. Side lighting provides illumination.

LEFT The bathroom alcove looks out over the garden and is defined by an architrave which matches those framing the double doorway and the washing alcove. Taps (faucets) and a diverter are mounted on the wall; water enters the tub from a filler at the side rather than from a conventional spout.

CASE STUDY **BATHROOM LIVING**

Built on a sand dune overlooking a beach, this South African holiday home was designed to echo the elemental qualities of its beautiful seaside setting. The point of reference for both architecture and decoration was the simplicity of vernacular fishermen's houses. The interior is largely open plan; in the master bedroom, a bathing area is minimally separated from the bed by an angled half-height partition so light, views, and sea breezes are uninterrupted throughout. The bathing area is treated as a wet room, with concrete floor and shower screened by a three-sided glass partition. In the sleeping area, the floor is wood. Colours and textures were chosen to promote a restful mood. The silvery leaves of the wild African olive trees that grow on the dunes inspired the use of silver-grey on the shutters and window frames. The bathtub is positioned in front of a large window with a view on to one of the house's double decks.

ABOVE The sides of the bathtub, a Starck design, are rendered in concrete to match the floor, a treatment which introduces a softer-looking texture in keeping with the overall decorative scheme. The freestanding mixer is also by Starck, as are the sink taps (faucets) and shower seen in the picture at right.
RIGHT The shower is semi-enclosed by three panels of glass. A pair of ceramic bowls are mounted on to a table, with a shelf underneath for storing towels and accessories.

LEFT Soft colours and matt textures evoke the seaside setting in which this home is situated. The exposed beams of the timber roof are painted chalky white. The shift in flooring material from wood in the sleeping area to concrete in the bathroom barely registers because the two materials are tonally very similar. Perhaps unusually, by far the greater floor area is devoted to the bathroom, with the sleeping area occupying not much more space than the bed.
BELOW The angled half-height concrete partition preserves the airy openness of the space, while serving to anchor the position of the bed in the layout.

FAMILY BATHROOMS

The essence of the family bathroom is that it is shared space
and, generally, although not exclusively, multigenerational.

This means that bathroom users will tend to have different physical requirements and abilities, and a degree of latitude will need to be built in to account for these differences.

When a bathroom is shared by family members, there will also inevitably be times of the day when bottlenecks are likely to occur, such as early morning when everyone is getting ready for work and school, and during the evening wind-down to bedtime. Doubling up facilities – a pair of sinks, a shower plus bath – can help to ease the strain.

Family life, however, is not static. Children grow at an alarming rate, and the toddler you once had to coax, bribe, or threaten into the bath will soon be a teenager forming an intimate relationship with the bathroom mirror behind a locked door. Flexibility is the key to ensuring the bathroom accommodates these changes of emphasis.

Siting

Shared bathrooms work best when space is generous. If you have the option to choose, it may well be worth devoting a large room to the purpose and making do with less space elsewhere. Small rooms often work surprisingly well as children's bedrooms, whereas a cramped family bathroom is fairly certain to be a daily aggravation for all concerned.

Access is also a critical factor. A democratic location, which can be reached easily by all the bathroom's users, is the ideal. When children are small, it is a good idea if the bathroom is fairly close to their room or rooms, and, if not on the same level, at least sited where there are the minimum number of stairs to negotiate. This will help to prevent night-time tumbles, as well as those other sorts of accidents that occur when a child in the early stages of toilet training just doesn't make it in time.

LEFT Particularly welcome in a family bathroom, double sinks help to ease pressure at busy times. Here, the same facility is offered by a generous trough-like sink mounted on wall-hung units and served by a pair of wall-mounted taps (faucets).

RIGHT This spacious family bathroom incorporates a laundry area. Painted tongue-and-groove boarding provides a practical wall finish and a visual break, making the high ceiling appear lower. A narrow built-in bench runs along two walls.

LEFT Large bathtubs, such as this double-ended claw-foot tub, provide enough room for shared bathtimes.
BELOW Glossy white timber boarding on the walls, around the bathtub, and on the floor enhances the sense of space. The wide surround to the tub makes a convenient perch for a supervising parent.
RIGHT A family bathroom with a sympathetic combination of materials: wooden bathtub, slate flooring, and a ceramic sink set on a wooden ledge. The vertical radiator doubles up as a heated towel rail.

Layout, fixtures, and fittings

A family bathroom, which needs to stay the course and work well for different age groups, is best kept as straightforward as possible. Focus on function and safety when it comes to planning the layout and choosing fixtures and fittings. It is often a good idea to base the layout around the position of the bathtub – you will need extra clearance around or alongside the tub for kneeling or bending over to supervise small children during bathtime. Opt for the biggest tub you can fit comfortably in the space; corner or oval-sided tubs often provide more generous accommodation than standard rectangular designs. Small children enjoy the sociability of a shared bath, and it certainly simplifies matters for parents, too. At the same time, make sure that the bathtub is not too deep – bending over a deep tub to bathe small children or lift them out is just asking for back trouble. Large or double showers are also a good idea.

You may be tempted by the cutting-edge chic of a stainless-steel bathtub or a glass sink, but bear in mind that these materials demand extra maintenance to keep their pristine appearance – and children are notoriously messy when it comes to basic ablutions. White acrylic or ceramic fixtures and fittings are much easier to clean. Rounded edges are safer than sharp corners, too, while thermostatic controls reduce the risk of scalding.

One advantage of a spacious family bathroom is that you can double up facilities to ease congestion at key points in the day, particularly those morning and bedtime rush hours. Double sinks mean that two children can tackle teeth brushing and face washing at the same time; a shower cubicle separate from the tub will also speed things up a bit. If you cannot accommodate extra fixtures in the space at your disposal, consider installing sinks in children's rooms or an additional shower cubicle in a laundry or utility area.

Family bathrooms are also good places to install laundry machines. It makes shorter work of a routine chore if you can strip muddy clothing off your budding sports star and pile it straight into the washing machine, rather than undertake endless trips to and fro between the dirty clothes basket

and utility room. In Britain, electrical points are prohibited in a bathroom, which means that the power supply for laundry machines must be routed through the wall and connected to an exterior switch. A stacked washing machine and dryer can be neatly enclosed inside a full-height cubicle.

Anyone who has ever ventured into a nursery or primary school bathroom and marvelled at the rows of Lilliputian toilets and sinks will appreciate that small children need assistance when it comes to accessing basic facilities. Standard toilets and sinks are too high for little children to reach by themselves. There are sinks available which are height-adjustable, but these fittings, specifically designed for those with special needs, are expensive. Far more straightforward is to provide booster steps to bring the child up to the right level. A more permanent arrangement would be to construct some form of stepped platform which could also double up as either seating or concealed storage.

Design and decoration

For many small children, bathing is simply a type of indoor water sport. Bearing this in mind, surfaces and finishes should be fully waterproof and easy to clean; they must also be non-slip as far as possible. Tongue-and-groove wood panelling, ceramic tiles, and mosaic tiles make practical wall cladding; linoleum, vinyl, cork, and rubber work well on the floor. Shiny, reflective surfaces such as glass, metal, and expanses of mirror will only demand additional upkeep. Even when children grow past the splashing stage, a family bathroom is still a shared space, which will necessitate a higher degree of maintenance than a bathroom used by only one person. To combat this, avoid fiddly detail, raised edges, or contours where grime can build up.

Resist the temptation to theme the bathroom in some form of child-centred way beyond what is both easy and economic to change. Vivid colour is always uplifting and has mileage; a novelty shower curtain can be replaced at a later date at little expense. More permanent themed features are best avoided. You can, for example, buy Disney-themed bathroom fittings and fixtures, everything from taps (faucets)

the handles of which are in the shape of mouse ears to toilets with seats that have the same familiar profile: aesthetics apart, the amusement factor will be short-lived.

Storage

To a large degree, the workability of a family bathroom will depend on adequate storage provision. It is not merely a question of making sure everyone has a place to put their toothbrush – other possessions, products, and accessories demand plenty of house room. When children are very small, bath toys are an important part of the whole bathing experience. Plastic mesh or string bags which allow toys to drain dry after use make good impromptu organizers;

generous ledges or margins around tubs can also be put to good use. You will need secure, lockable storage for bleach, bathroom cleansers, and other products; medicine cabinets should be positioned well out of reach and should also be kept locked. Keep the first-aid box well out of children's reach but unlocked, so that its contents can be readily accessed in case of emergency.

The need for storage becomes no less acute when your children enter adolescence and grooming products take over from rubber ducks and toy submarines. Shampoos, lotions, body scrubs, and other potions tend to proliferate – as is the case with breakfast cereals, many will be tried and few will be completely used up. Instigate periodic clean-out sessions.

ABOVE FAR LEFT A small stool or play chair provides an extra boost to help children reach the sink. Rolled towels are stored in a wire basket for easy access. Tongue-and-groove boarding is a practical wall covering. **LEFT** Flooring in family bathrooms and wet areas should be as non-slip as possible. Matt-surfaced ceramic tiles are better than those with a glossier finish. **ABOVE LEFT** Built-in bathroom storage keeps accessories and linen to hand. The 'red cross' cabinet provides an accent of colour and a touch of humour. **ABOVE RIGHT** Alessi accessories, including the 'flowerpot' toilet brush, add a playful quality in a family bathroom, as do the pink mosaic and lime-green perspex storage units.

CASE STUDY **THE FAMILY BATHROOM**

RIGHT The shower area is completely tiled in blue mosaic; water drains directly to the floor.
BELOW A bathroom that includes laundry facilities as well as storage space for clothes simplifies family life. Dirty clothes can go straight into the washing machine, clean clothes straight into the cupboards.
BELOW RIGHT The laboratory-style sink is deep enough for handwashing delicate items of clothing. The 'swing' taps (faucets) are easy for young fingers to manipulate.

For one Danish family, the opportunity arose to achieve a large, inclusive bathroom when a basement area was undergoing substantial renovation. Their brief to a firm of interior designers was to create a family bathroom where the laundry could be done at the same time as children were supervised in the tub. Two rooms in the basement were transformed into a linked bathroom/laundry and shower room. The larger of the two (17m²/183sq ft) includes a bathtub, washing machine, and dryer along one wall. To keep the bedrooms free of clothes, the opposite wall is fitted with cupboards that house the entire family's wardrobe. The cupboards, although extensive, have frosted-glass doors which make them appear much less dominant. The smaller room (6.5m²/70sq ft), accessed by a revolving door also in frosted glass, is treated like a wet room, with an open double shower occupying the end wall. The result is a supremely functional space, where practicality is matched by simple good looks.

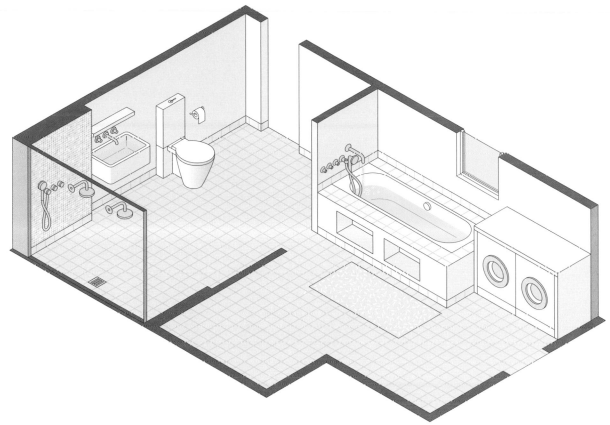

ABOVE The two interconnecting rooms are separated from each other by a revolving door.

LEFT The floor throughout both of the adjoining bathrooms is cream-coloured ceramic tile, laid over underfloor heating. Plastered walls are painted with a special bathroom paint designed to be used in areas of high humidity. Pegs for towels are located near the bathtub.

RIGHT A large tub is ideal for shared bathtimes. This tub has a tiled surround that matches the floor and incorporates two large niches, ideal for stowing bathmats, towels, and other accessories. Wall-mounted fixtures keep the area around the bath clear.

LEFT Bathtubs can be slotted into areas where there is not full head height for standing room and moving about. Thin tiles of beautiful mottled-blue limestone clad this bathtub and the wall behind it. A wall-mounted radiator makes good use of the available space.

BELOW An alcove in a guest bedroom has been fitted out as a washing area, with a deep Belfast sink inset into a panelled cabinet. Slips of marble serve as a splashback.

RIGHT The graphic angles and planes of this shower room are picked out in strong colour: vivid yellow behind the sink and black ceramic tile on the floor and shower area. An etched-glass partition serves as a shower screen and reduces a closed-in feeling for bathers.

AWKWARD SPACES

There are occasions when there is no other option but to site a bathroom in an area which is irregularly or awkwardly shaped.

A sloping ceiling, a beam or column that can't be moved, tight corners and angles – all can cause a bit of a headache when it comes to planning a workable layout.

Integrating the necessary fixtures and fittings within an awkward layout can amount to something of a three-dimensional jigsaw puzzle. The problem may need to be tackled on two fronts. First, it's a question of analysing the space so that apparent drawbacks are neutralized or even turned to your advantage. Secondly, you may well find that specially designed tubs, sinks, and toilets will help you to overcome spatial anomalies.

If awkward layouts create difficulties when it comes to design and function, they can be visually jarring, too. A regular shape is inherently more relaxing and easier on the eye than one which is asymmetric or which has odd angles and corners. Various decorative strategies can be adopted as remedial measures to overcome the problem or simply to draw attention away from such features.

ABOVE The otherwise redundant area underneath the stairs has been fitted out as a bathroom, with a sink inset into a counter. The open treads on the lower stairs allow light through.

RIGHT An angled layout is sometimes unavoidable. There are sinks and toilets designed to fit into corners; an alternative, as here, is to fit the space out as neatly as possible. A dummy wall accommodating a back-to-the-wall pan turns the corner to serve as a unit for the inset sink.

FAR RIGHT Full head height is not necessary for all bathroom activities, but it must be possible to stand in front of the sink without banging your head on the ceiling. In this attic conversion, the sink has been positioned under the window set into the plane of the roof. A mirror on a concertina arm is fixed to the side of the recess.

Sloping ceilings

Bathrooms tucked under the eaves – in a converted attic space, for example – can make good use of floor area which is otherwise redundant because of lack of head height. Provided there is enough space to manoeuvre yourself into a tub without cracking your head on a beam, a bathtub can usefully be sited where a ceiling drops down; so, too, can a toilet, as long as there is head height, or standing room, in front. The area immediately in front of a dormer window, where there is both head height and natural light, can be a good position for a sink

Installing a sunken bath is another way of overcoming lack of head height. Sinking a bath into the floor as opposed to sinking it within a purpose-built platform does, however, have structural implications. The last thing you want is to crash through to the room below, bathtub and all, in the middle of your ablutions. You will need expert advice from a qualified surveyor to check that there is adequate support available for the weight of a bathtub filled with water; the load must be correctly distributed through the bathroom floor and on to the load-bearing (usually external) wall. Floor joists may need to be strengthened by doubling up to bear the additional weight of a sunken tub.

Low or sloping ceilings can feel oppressive. Bouncing light off the ceiling plane with an uplighter can help to increase the sense of volume.

Angles and corners

Areas where walls do not meet at right angles or which include unmovable piers or structural supports present a definite challenge when it comes to layout. If the room is spacious, the simplest and neatest solution can be to straighten the angles by building out from the walls to form a regular shape within the irregular one – or even a circular enclosure. This strategy, of course, entails the loss of some floor area, but it may be a sacrifice well worth making. Such fitted spaces also provide the opportunity to conceal toilet cisterns and other visible plumbing within the panelling, along with storage facilities.

Where angles are simply unavoidable, you may be able to accommodate them with angled fixtures such as offset corner sinks and bathtubs. Toilets which fit into corners are also available; the key consideration here is making sure there is room for the legs on either side. Some corner and standard toilets come with seats that can be angled left or right, which can help if leg room is a potential problem. Interlocking bath and shower cubicles are other fixtures that make good spatial use of a corner.

Ingenious layout and clever fixtures are not the only things that help with difficult spaces. Decoration can also distract the eye from awkward angles or corners. Spatial irregularities will be less noticeable when bathrooms are white or a single colour, or uniformly tiled and clad, than when different surfaces are picked out in contrasting tones or materials.

Long, narrow spaces

In narrow locations, such as bathrooms created out of former corridors, aligning fixtures along one wall is probably the best design solution. This keeps access and circulation routes clear and avoids difficult bottlenecks where, for example, you might otherwise have to squeeze round the corner of a sink in order to climb into the bathtub. The great advantage of such in-line layouts is that they simplify plumbing runs considerably, which means that the result not only will look neater, but will be less expensive to achieve as well. Provided you do not compromise practicality unnecessarily, opting for a narrow sink and tub can ease the pressure on space when dealing with a long, narrow space.

When fixtures are lined up along one wall, it is important to provide a degree of separation between the toilet and sink and bath. A half-height partition will give the necessary physical and psychological separation without blocking light or detracting from the overall sense of space. Wall-hung toilets, bidets, and sinks enhance the sense of space by keeping the floor area clear.

A door which opens inwards can be an obstruction in a narrow bathroom. To overcome this, consider replacing the door with a sliding panel or rehanging it so that it opens the other way. The 'free' wall opposite the main bathroom fixtures can be fitted with a low, narrow bench or ledge with storage space underneath or a row of pegs above. Greater visual breadth can be suggested by covering one or both walls with an expanse of mirror.

Narrow spaces, particularly if they have been created by partitioning a bigger room, sometimes appear disproportionately high. If you are faced with this problem, lowering the ceiling can help to adjust proportions and also provides an opportunity to fit recessed lighting. Large, square floor tiles will increase the sense of breadth.

ABOVE Changes in level can help to address the disadvantages of narrow layouts. Here, a bath sunk into a platform is minimally partitioned from a shower area at the far end. Keeping to the same colour and material for all surfaces and finishes is another good strategy for overcoming spatial limitations. RIGHT In this extremely narrow space, the textured indigo walls provide a soothing, uniform backdrop. Sink and toilet are aligned along one wall, with the cylindrical sink set into the end of a tapering built-in unit. At the far end is a sunken bath and shower.

RIGHT The Jacuzzi tub, clad in wood, is situated along the wall where head height drops down under the slope of the roof. A wall-hung toilet and bidet are positioned along the solid wall, with the shower tucked into the corner. The wooden shower tray was specially designed. The bathroom's flooring is teak decking; teak is a highly water-resistant wood. Glass is much too slippery to be used as flooring in an area which is likely to become wet.

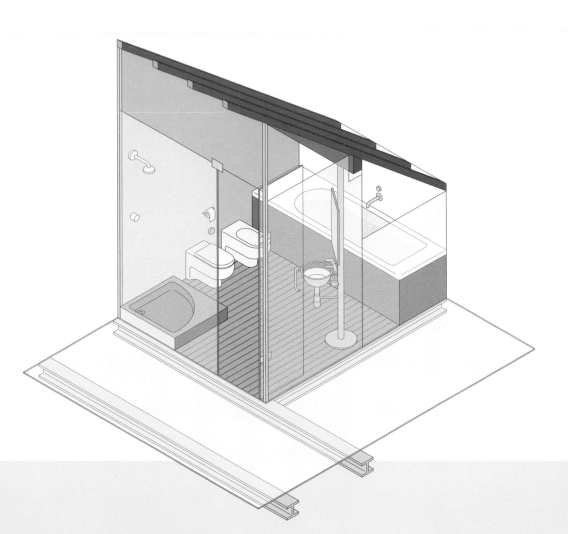

CASE STUDY **THE AWKWARD SPACE**

A loft-style approach to space planning was adopted in the conversion of this small house in the centre of Milan. Rather than keeping the existing partitions, the entire building was opened up, top to bottom, to create one space. The lower level is entirely open plan, accommodating cooking, eating, and living areas. A mezzanine level was slotted in above, providing just enough space for a bedroom and bathroom to be tucked under the eaves.

Extensive use of glass maintains the home's sense of volume and allows natural light to spill through from one area to another. While a combination of clear and frosted glass is employed to enclose the bathroom, glass features more dramatically as the flooring for the bedroom area, comprising about 25m² (269sq ft) in total. The result is both a minimal interruption of views throughout the space as a whole and an almost theatrical experience of being suspended in mid air.

LEFT AND ABOVE Glass suitable for flooring is thick annealed float glass. Here, it provides the dizzy sense of walking on air and reveals the underlying structure of steel beams. Two types of glass are used to enclose the bathroom: frosted glass to over head height to provide privacy and clear glass above. A skylight is positioned in the plane of the roof, between the exposed wooden beams. The orange wall that runs behind the shower, toilet, and bidet was painted with water-resistant paint and varnished for additional waterproofing.

FAR LEFT As wall space is limited, the sink is a special type serviced via a pipe that also acts as a supporting column.

SMALL BATHROOMS

While bathroom size may be on the increase – and most people's dream
bathroom will certainly be spacious – all too often reality falls short of the ideal.

If your bathroom more than merits the 'smallest room' tag, it need not disappoint you in other respects. Small can be functional – and even beautiful if you approach its design in the right manner and with appropriate forethought.

In cases where small means downright minute, you will have to accept that you simply can't have it all. Spend some time thinking carefully about your needs and preferences. Assessment is always an important part of the design process. When space is strictly limited, it's even more crucial than ever. Which features and fixtures could you do without? Which are absolutely essential? Double sinks are inevitably out of the question when there's barely room for one, and you may well find that a bidet is surplus to requirements if it's going to be a squeeze merely siting the toilet so that its position is practical. Showers are certainly more space saving than bathtubs, but don't automatically assume that just because your bathroom is small you have to forgo a tub. If you prefer bathing to showering and if a long, hot soak is a key element of your daily routine, it would be a mistake to choose greater floor area over the opportunity to relax the way you want to. Substituting a shower for a bath may also affect the resale value of your home, so bear this in mind. If you do choose to install a bath, you can always include an overbath shower as well.

Clever spatial planning allied with compact fixtures and features will maximize the area at your disposal. Equally important is adopting decorative strategies that enhance the sense of space, rather than contributing further to the lack of it. However small it might be, there is no reason why a bathroom should feel confining. All it takes to avoid a cramped and claustrophobic result is the correct approach.

Layout, fixtures, and fittings

When you're tackling the design of a small bathroom, the first step is to investigate whether it is possible to increase the floor area, even if only by a small margin. A matter of millimetres may not sound like much, but it can make all the difference between discomfort and ease of use. Partition walls can be brought forwards into hallways or connecting areas with relatively little disruption, or there may be an adjacent cupboard which can be annexed.

If you cannot increase the floor area, you may be able to maximize usable wall space. Consider blocking up one of a pair of windows, for example, in order to squeeze in a shower or a heated towel rail. A door that opens inwards can be rehung to open the other way or replaced by a sliding panel or screen. Bifold or sliding shower screens also save space.

Many contemporary manufacturers produce ranges of compact fixtures designed for minuscule bathrooms and cloakrooms. Such fixtures range from smaller-than-standard models to those which are shaped to make the best use of space. Research the market before you commit yourself. In a small bathroom, common sense would dictate that the bathtub should be positioned on the longest wall: indeed, you may assume you have little choice in the matter. But short, wide baths and baths shaped so that they taper at the

ABOVE Small wall-mounted sinks, together with wall-mounted taps (faucets), make good use of limited space. RIGHT This small bathroom in a Tuscan farmhouse appears larger because the view across the floor is not interrupted by the sides of a bathtub. Instead, the tub is sunken, with pale-grey mosaic tiling unifying the entire area into a cohesive whole.

ABOVE A pivoting glass shower door takes up less floor space than a hinged version would.
LEFT Custom-made floor-to-ceiling concealed storage cupboards make the most of available space and reduce clutter. The built-in storage wall accommodates a wall-hung toilet and inset radiator. Open niches provide room for display, while a slim modern unit under the sink is used to house everyday necessities.
RIGHT A gridded teak panel serves as a shower tray slotted over the top of a sunken bath.
FAR RIGHT A partition separates the bathtub from the toilet. Shower controls are mounted directly on to the surface; a narrow slit allows light through.

foot end may allow you to fit a tub across the width of the room, thus freeing space for other fixtures. Tapered baths are available in left- and right-hand versions. Corner baths, sinks, and shower stalls can also help when space is limited.

Human parameters being what they are, however, there is a limit to how far bathroom fixtures can be miniaturized and remain comfortable and functional. If you're tall, a short bath won't accommodate your frame; sitz baths, where you sit rather than lie prone, aren't for everyone. I personally prefer baths to showers and once arrived at a hotel desperate for a long soak. Unfortunately, the bathtub was a sitz tub. Seeking full immersion, I sat in it the wrong way round – and got stuck.

Small sinks are generally more successful than small tubs. Those which have integral surrounds, where you can

place soap and so on, obviate the need for a shelf. Bear in mind that if the sink is very small and shallow you will not be able to fit a shelf above it without running the risk of hitting your head every time you bend over the sink. But small sinks aren't always the answer; sometimes a different shape will do the trick. Simply choosing a round sink rather than an oval or oblong one can prevent the type of awkward layout where the sink overhangs the bath.

Because they keep the floor area free, wall-hung sinks, toilets, and bidets make good sense in a small bathroom. You will need to ensure, however, that the structure of the wall can bear the weight. Back-to-the-wall toilets mean that the cistern is hidden behind a dummy panel, which gives a seamless look and provides the opportunity to make

recessed shelves or concealed storage. Sinks and bathtubs with internally illuminated plastic walls which make them appear to 'float' also increase the sense of visual lightness, as do fixtures made of glass. Showers which are screened by glass partitions preserve light and views; even better than this are frameless showers enclosed in glass.

Underfloor heating is space saving. Alternatively, opt for wall-mounted heated towel rails or radiators. Wall-mounted taps (faucets) are also neater looking; monomixers take up less space than a pair of taps; built-in shower valves give a cleaner design. Efficient ventilation is particularly essential in a small area, where damp and odours can build up. An extractor activated by a light switch is often a good idea.

Design and decoration

As a general rule, small spaces seem bigger when the decoration is kept simple and coordinated. This does not necessarily mean restricting your choice to all-white, but single colour schemes or schemes where colours are tonally very close do tend to work best. Extend tiling or other forms of cladding to cover whole walls, rather than break up the surface unnecessarily. Junctions and edges where one material or surface meets another are always very important; in a small bathroom it is crucial that these should be as neat and inconspicuous as possible. Mirror, of course, is another tried and tested way of amplifying the sense of space. A sheet of mirror placed opposite a window or mirrors on opposite walls bounce light around. Installing spotlights or tiny, recessed fixtures around the perimeter of the room will give the feeling of extra breadth and height.

In a small space, clutter is anathema. Restrict what is kept out on view to the bare necessities and exploit every opportunity for built-in storage. Separate shelves and cabinets can begin to encroach on space; sleek units built in under built-ins or around other fixtures have a more considered look and can accommodate a wide range of possessions, from bathroom cleansers and other practical necessities to cosmetics and linen. If space is really tight, you can fit a towel rail or pegs to the back of the door.

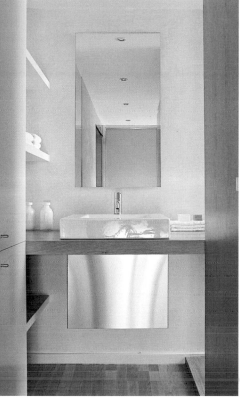

ABOVE Reflective surfaces and finishes make the most of available light. White-painted walls, the sheet of mirror over the sink, and the shiny metallic finish of the wall-hung unit all serve to enhance the sense of space, rather than diminish it.

LEFT Simplicity of detailing cuts down on visual distraction. The shower area, draining directly to the floor, is tiled in blue mosaic and minimally separated from the rest of the bathroom by a frameless glass screen.

RIGHT Mirror is an excellent device for multiplying views and making a space seem bigger than it really is. Here, a panel of mirror behind the shower and bathtub reflects the garden view; glass partitions don't block light.

LEFT This cloakroom has been neatly fitted out with wall-hung toilet and sink.

RIGHT Wood panelling encloses a cloakroom that has been slotted into an understairs space and minimizes the effect of the angled planes.

BELOW Guest cloakrooms often provide the excuse for a little decorative whimsy.

Cloakrooms

The smallest of small rooms, the cloakroom may present a double whammy when it comes to layout, often being both restricted in size and tucked into an awkward spot. A popular site for a ground-floor cloakroom tends to be under the stairs. Today's compact fixtures mean that it is not difficult to convert what virtually amounts to a broom cupboard into a guest loo. A small wall-hung sink and wall-hung toilet, along with a radiator or heated towel rail, will provide sufficient facilities for what usually only amounts to short stays. Many people relish the opportunity to make a style statement in

a guest toilet that they would not make elsewhere in the home; a sink in the form of a small glass bowl, which may not be practical for frequent use, can work well here.

Cloakroom decor has traditionally been of the self-mocking or light-hearted variety: framed cartoons, old school photographs, and collages of ephemera seem to be irresistible in this context. A little wit and humour never go amiss, but do make an attempt to keep muddy boots and other paraphernalia somewhere else. A cloakroom converted from a broom cupboard is one thing; a cloakroom that still looks like a broom cupboard is not a very hospitable place.

CASE STUDY **THE SMALL BATHROOM**

Clean lines and clever detailing make the most of this small guest bathroom, located on the top floor of a new-build house in London. Although the bathroom is only 1.3m (4ft 3in) by 4m (13ft) in size, the overall mood is one of spaciousness and tranquillity. Matt, neutral surfaces and soft, diffused light echo the reticent decorative approach taken elsewhere in the house.

The custom-made bath/walk-in shower can comfortably accommodate two people and measures 2m (6½ft) from the angled back rest to the glass side. The same matt ceramic tiles used to form the base of the bath extend to form the main bathroom flooring, helping the space to read as a whole. Similarly, the wall-hung toilet and sink keep the floor area clear. In a small space, it is important to reduce clutter to a minimum. Here, storage units recessed into the walls are concealed by mirrored fronts. Under the ceramic sink, a box-like construction clad in stainless steel hides supporting brackets and pipework.

ABOVE AND LEFT The walls of the bathroom are tanked with waterproof render over a waterproof fibreglass layer. The soft, matt appearance of this finish echoes the unglazed ceramic tile used both to line the tub and as the main bathroom flooring. The side of the bathtub is a sheet of toughened safety glass, held in position by channels set into the walls and the floor. The joints are sealed with a high-performance waterproof sealant of the type used in aquaria.

LEFT AND BELOW The bathroom is located on the top floor of the house and looks out over a roof terrace. The window is a frosted frosted double-glazed unit in a galvanized steel frame. The bath's size means that there is no need for a screen between the shower and the rest of the bathroom – this preserves important in a small bathroom.

WET ROOMS

Wet rooms are essentially walk-in showers writ large, or at least larger, a natural progression from floor-draining showers or showers without trays.

While there remains something of a grey area between a wet room and a large walk-in shower, wet rooms are usually defined as fully waterproofed areas where the walls of the bathroom form the boundaries of the shower itself. Wet rooms typically include a sink and toilet; there may or may not be a bathtub as well. Essential is good water pressure, such as that provided by a power shower: the wet room is not the place for a dribbling, intermittent trickle.

In recent years, the wet room has emerged as a definitive trend in bathroom design, and there are several reasons for this rise in popularity. One is undoubtedly speed: busy people who prefer a no-nonsense and quick route to getting clean often find that a wet room provides the requisite efficiency – not to mention the bonus of making short work of maintenance. Then there is the spatial aspect: wet rooms make sense where space is limited or, indeed, awkwardly shaped because there are few fixtures and fittings to take up floor area. At the same time, those who have only a small space at their disposal but find that the full blast of a power shower means that water would otherwise spray everywhere may find a wet room the only practical option. Equally persuasive is the feeling of liberation. A wet room provides the type of unfettered contact with water that a more furnished and fitted bathroom can lack. No more awkward

ABOVE Changes of level can be very effective in wet rooms, helping to define different areas of activity. The shower area seen here is raised up a couple of steps from the rest of the bathroom.

LEFT Teak and certain other hardwoods are water-resistant enough to serve as flooring in wet areas, provided the water is allowed to drain away. This wooden floor is slatted so that water does not remain lying on the surface.

RIGHT This wet room features both a shower and a bathtub. The long towel rail doubles up as a grab rail for safe access to the tub. Mosaic, because of the tight nature of the grid in which it is laid, provides better grip underfoot than larger tiles.

or claustrophobic shower cubicles to negotiate, no more clinging shower curtains. On the downside, the need for full waterproofing imposes certain constraints in terms of siting and can also lead to greater expense.

The first wet room I ever saw, years before such an arrangement became fashionable, was at the home of a sculptor friend who at that time was living in what amounted to a derelict castle. He had taken a big room and clad it entirely in terrazzo with underfloor heating. The shower was a pipe jutting from the wall, and the drain was in the centre of the floor. The result had all the elemental appeal of today's sleek variations on the same theme.

Siting

Turning a bathroom into a wet room makes perfect sense if the space is small or awkwardly shaped, or both. You can also convert part of an existing sleeping area to form a wet room, provided you install a partition of some type between the wet and dry areas. A wet room makes a compact supplement to a main bathroom and as such can be slotted in where plumbing and structural considerations permit.

Wet rooms obviously need thorough waterproofing, which in turn may require the use of dense materials such as stone or tile. Check with a surveyor to establish whether your chosen site is appropriate or the existing floor structure will need to be strengthened. A concrete subfloor provides a stable base for wet-room construction. Wooden floor structures may be subject to movement, which can lead to cracking and the risk of water penetration. For this reason, it can be easier to install a wet room on the ground floor.

You may also need to consult your local water authority about water pressure. Power or hydromassage showers need a certain level of mains pressure to work, one which is normally well within the range which water providers are obliged to supply. However, in some areas, if water pressure does drop below what is regarded as an adequate level, whether it be because of leaks, floods, or other problems in the supply, your shower may cease to work and you may in turn have little ground for compensation.

Layout, fixtures, and fittings

Existing plumbing and drainage arrangements will probably be the most important factor determining layout. Unless you include a tub, too, there are fewer fixed points that need to be fitted into the space. Rectilinear layouts are not the only solution: showers, and hence wet rooms, lend themselves to curved enclosures, which generate more spatial interest from both within and without.

Shower fixtures can be positioned in a corner, in the middle of a wall, freestanding, or centrally and overhead. Wall-hung sinks and toilets will keep the floor area of the wet room clear and also allow surfaces to be cleaned and hosed down easily. Accentuate the Zen-like appeal with minimal fixtures and fittings.

There is a huge range of shower fixtures to choose from (see pages 154–9), with respect not only to appearance, but also to performance and special features. Thermostatic controls which are easy to operate are essential, particularly if young children will be using the wet room, in order to avoid scalds; controls should be positioned away from the shower head so that you can test the temperature before you step under the water. Massaging jets and other spa-type features multiply the enjoyment. A built-in waterproof bench or seat is a good idea if you like to take your time showering.

Wet rooms are miserable if they are cold; underfloor heating is one of the most practical ways of warming the space. Wall-mounted radiators or heated towel rails can also be installed. It is vital that all electrical work is carried out by a qualified professional, as wet rooms multiply the risk of water coming into lethal contact with electricity.

A small wet room is not the place for storage because of the risk of soaking, and you may have to keep even towels elsewhere; in larger areas, storage can be fitted in well away from the shower where splashes are less likely to occur.

ABOVE Water is an important element in the work of British-based architect Seth Stein. In this new-build house in the Toronto suburbs, a semicircular concrete partition sweeps around a large wet area. RIGHT The houses that Rick Joy, an architect based in Tucson, Arizona, has designed in the southwestern desert place the timeless qualities of space, light, and nature at the centre of the picture. This elemental wet room, with its glass wall and concrete floor, makes a sensuous contrast to the dry desert landscape.

ABOVE LEFT Although wet rooms are a recent trend, and are often associated with contemporary design, this example in a French country house proves that the rustic look can be equally successful. Plain rendered walls surround a tiled sunken shower area. **ABOVE RIGHT** A teak-lined wet room has a warm, enclosing feel. Grooves between the slatted timbers on the floor drain water away. **RIGHT** A custom-made wet room features a concrete trough designed by the owner. The minimal shower fittings are a pair of 'Pipe' designs by Boffi.

Waterproofing

The greatest practical challenge is creating a room which is fully waterproof. You need to make absolutely sure that there is no risk of water penetrating into the structure of your house, where it could cause damp and dry rot.

Waterproofing is not simply a question of cladding walls and floors with an impervious material. The existing underlying wall and floor structure may well need additional waterproofing as well. This can take the form of 'tanking', which consists of applying a bituminous waterproof layer or a polythene membrane before installing final surfaces and finishes; you may also need to line walls and floor with marine ply. Grouting between tiles or mosaic must be carefully applied to ensure there are no gaps.

Water penetration is more likely to occur if water remains standing on the surface. For this reason, floors should slope gently to the drain, which is often positioned in the centre of the room. For a more minimal and elegant effect, flooring – especially floors made of large stone slabs or tiles – can be designed so that grooves or channels drain water away.

Waterproofing is much easier if the subfloor is concrete. Alternatively, a wet floor can be constructed by having a shower tray made from a single piece of stone, grooved or sloped to a drainage point. This can be installed over a metal tray to catch any seepage. The remainder of the floor can then be tiled with stone to match.

Surfaces and finishes

In the case of wet rooms, decoration is largely a matter of material choice. Whatever material you choose should have high water resistance; in the context of flooring, it should also be as non-slip as possible.

Various types of stone, including limestone, slate, and marble, are popular choices for wet-room cladding, but even marine ply can be used if it is properly sealed. Mosaic and ceramic tile offer the potential for strong colour. Partition walls can be made of glass brick, frosted glass, or high-tech glass which turns from clear to opaque at the touch of a switch. Waterproofed recessed spotlights set into the ceiling or floor, or both, dispel any hint of confinement.

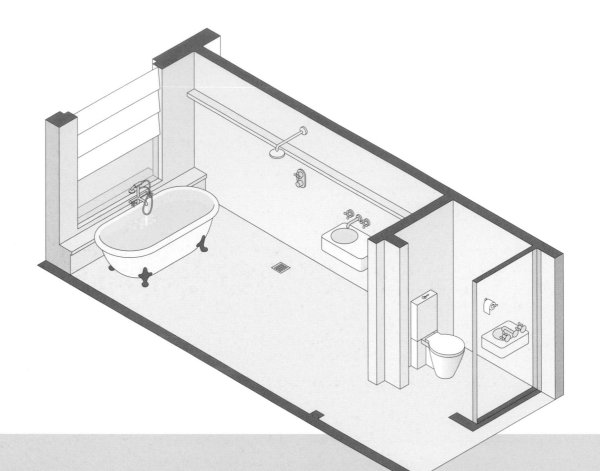

LEFT To help to maintain the sense that the bathroom is a room in its own right, the toilet is sited separately, partitioned from the main space.

BELOW The tub is a traditional rolltop design with ornate claw feet painted matt black. The taps (faucets) and shower set are floor-mounted. A specially made steel towel rail extends along the full length of the wall.

CASE STUDY **THE WET ROOM**

The wet room is a fairly recent development and, as such, tends to be associated with cutting-edge design. But the same basic approach also works with more traditional fittings and fixtures, providing a sympathetic blend of old and new. The overall design brief for the renovation of this 1920s townhouse in Amsterdam was to improve spatial quality and put a fresh face on things without losing the spirit of the existing architecture.

The wet room serves as the main family bathroom and is located next to the master bedroom. Neither the client nor the architect engaged on the renovation wanted to encroach on the space by enclosing the shower in a separate cubicle, so the wet room approach was the obvious solution. The bulk of the work was to make the room fully waterproof. This entailed reinforcing existing wooden beams with a concrete slab laid over the top. The luminous, lively surfaces have a subtle quality all their own.

ABOVE The sink is a simple wall-mounted ceramic design, with wall-mounted taps (faucets). **LEFT** The floor and wall behind the shower head are finished in white marble terrazzo. Standard terrazzo incorporates quite large pieces of marble; in this version, the marble fragments are very fine, which meant the cement in the terrazzo mix had to be treated in a special way. The first attempt at the finish did not work and it had to be redone. The other walls and ceiling are finished with a water-resistant, 'breathing' latex, a rubberized treatment that absorbs surface water. A long shelf, or 'plank', provides space to store accessories.

LEFT Pod-like enclosures can be a good solution for separating bathrooms from other areas in a multipurpose space such as a loft. This simple, box-like structure houses a shower and sink. The vibrant yellow interior contrasts with the bright blue used to pick out the exterior.

RIGHT AND BELOW Even more eye-catching than the example at left is this curved bathroom pod clad in perspex. Coloured panels enliven the enclosure from outside and in. The pod is located near the kitchen for simplicity of servicing. The curved form makes dynamic use of a corner.

BATHROOM PODS

Bathroom pods are freestanding enclosures housing fixtures and fittings within a larger area or open-plan space.

At its simplest, a bathroom pod can be a prefabricated shower cubicle. More all-encompassing are purpose-built modules containing sinks, showers, bathtubs, and toilets.

The bathroom pod largely owes its existence to the type of free-form planning made possible by the wide, open spaces of a loft. In many loft conversions, servicing arrangements are grouped in a central core; alternatively, there may be a choice of servicing points. When it comes to determining the layout of the space as a whole, it therefore makes practical and economic sense to start with the fixed elements of kitchen and bathroom, and to keep these areas as closely linked as possible.

Although it is true that bathroom pods are designed to provide private, intimate spaces for bodily functions, their obvious prominence, especially where surrounding areas are otherwise open plan, leave one in no doubt as to their purpose. While you may be perfectly relaxed about such an arrangement, visitors to your home may find the experience of stepping into what resembles a space-age street convenience rather more challenging.

Prefabricated pods

Prefabricated modules range from basic shower cubicles to fully plumbed, fitted, and finished bathroom pods manufactured specially for use in hotels, apartments, and other large-scale developments. In the latter case, the pods are delivered to site. Once they have been lifted into position by crane, it is a quick and simple matter to make the appropriate service connections. While these types of bathroom pod are not generally applicable for the individual or domestic market, the increasing trend for prefabrication in the construction industry may well see such modules become a feasible option for new-build or home-extension projects in the not too distant future.

At the other end of the scale are prefabricated shower cubicles or cabinets which enclose the shower within a single freestanding, sealed unit. Walls, roof, and floor may be moulded in one piece for total waterproofing; in some designs, roofs can be opened for ventilation or closed to retain heat and steam. Many roofs are either transparent or opaline to counter any sense of confinement. Provided plumbing connections are easy to make, such cubicles can be positioned virtually anywhere. The designs available range from basic and often rather cramped cabinets to more luxurious versions with the latest spa features, from massaging jets, to steam, to chromatherapy. Some even incorporate a clock, alarm, and stereo radio, along with an integral cabinet for bathrobes and towels.

Despite the all-singing, all-dancing specifications, however, many prefabricated cubicles still leave a lot to be desired in terms of aesthetics – although this may change as they become more popular. And there are exceptions. One particularly sleek steam bath capsule, which was designed by Norman Foster, has integral seating, overhead and handheld showers, and side jets.

Purpose-built pods

Positioning of the bathroom pod, particularly where other areas are more or less completely open plan, is critical. Although the scale of the pod may entail only a relatively small loss of floor area, the enclosure should be constructed where it will not create dead, unusable space surrounding it. Think about circulation routes and the flow of activity from area to area. The site of a pod can usefully demarcate public zones for living, eating, and cooking from more private enclaves such as sleeping or working areas.

There is no restriction when it comes to style or material if a bathroom pod or enclosure is purpose-built. However, such freestanding designs generally work best where there is plenty of ceiling height. The spatial volume offered by a typical high-ceilinged or double-height loft is ideal because there is no risk that the pod will interrupt views to the extent

LEFT Like window seats or curtained beds, pods have a perennial appeal which is all the more heightened where space is otherwise free-form. This curved structure, faced in textured render, includes its own 'threshold', which reinforces the sense of stepping into a private world. Inside, the pod features a large circular stainless-steel bath and a curtained shower. **ABOVE** Less a private world and more a piece of domestic equipment, this bathroom capsule has a curved hinged door. The base is a concrete slab; fixtures are simple and utilitarian.

that the entire space stops reading as a whole. Where rooms or areas are more conventionally scaled, on the other hand, a pod can sometimes look a little uncomfortable. Raising a pod or enclosure a little way off the ground and lighting the base will make it appear to hover, which is another way of maintaining a sense of visual lightness.

The shape of the enclosure can be rectilinear and boxy, or curved like a futuristic capsule. Bear in mind that straight lines and right angles are on the whole cheaper and easier to construct and make the placement of fittings and fixtures less problematic. On the other hand, curved enclosures have innate sculptural appeal and particularly suit showers.

Bathroom pods are usually visible from all sides, so it is important that they look as good on the outside as they do on the inside. A balance should also be struck between preserving light and views, and providing necessary privacy. Translucent materials such as frosted glass, glass brick, and perspex, particularly when coloured, help to transform such features into glowing focal points.

ABOVE A shower is neatly integrated into a loft. Its flanking walls form part of a partition that doubles as a headboard-cum-spatial-divider. A sheet of glass serves as a transparent screen, while a washing area, fitted with sinks, is plumbed outside the shower enclosure.

RIGHT A variation on a similar theme encloses a shower in a glass box like an overscaled, off-the-peg cubicle. Other bathroom facilities, including a pair of sinks and a freestanding tub, are located outside the box.

CASE STUDY **THE BATHROOM POD**

Loft living has set the seal on transformable, flexible space – homes where there are no conventionally assigned areas or rooms, but which can change according to need or preference. This loft, situated in an old quarter of Barcelona, pushes the notion of flexibility to the limit, with its sliding partitions and mobile storage units that can be pushed out of the way when not required. As in more conventional surroundings, the bathroom remains a fixed point by virtue of its necessary connections to servicing. Here, that necessity has been boldly expressed by siting the bathroom at the core of the space in an enclosed cube, like a pod or a house within a house.

ABOVE The bathroom 'pod' or enclosure sits in the middle of the loft, between the cooking/eating/working area and a sleeping area at the rear. An opaque glass sliding panel provides privacy without blocking out the light. The restored wooden beams are all that remain of the building's history. Other materials are determinedly hard-edged and industrial: the floor throughout is concrete and the stair and mezzanine walkway are steel.
RIGHT The bathroom enclosure is the only space which has been treated like a room. The rest of the loft can be configured in different ways by means of a system of built-in cupboards, pull-down blinds, sliding panels, and movable units.

ABOVE In keeping with the industrial aesthetic, fixtures are simple and functional. Opposite the metal-clad bath, a shower drains directly to the floor – the raised lip of the surrounding framework prevents the water from spilling out.

RIGHT The bathroom pod forms a separate enclosure at the heart of the open-plan space.

HOME SPAS

Today, the sensory experience and benefits of the spa are no longer
limited to trips to a gym or health club, or a stay at a health retreat.

Just as kitchen design has been revolutionized over the past few decades by absorbing influences from professional examples outside the domestic realm, so, too, bathrooms are increasingly sporting the fixtures and fittings that are more typically associated with upmarket gyms, health clubs, and wellness centres. Baths and showers with high-tech features such as chromatherapy, massaging jets, ultrasound, and even built-in music systems turn an everyday routine into the height of pampered indulgence.

Such multisensory experience does not come cheap — although neither does a day at a health club. If you regularly visit a spa, it can be cost effective over the long run to install such state-of-the-art features in your home. But bear in mind that a single fixture, such as a high-spec shower, can cost the equivalent of an entire bathroom's worth of standard fixtures. In many cases, the home spa will also be a fully appointed fitness room, incorporating exercise machines for a thorough workout before more passive water therapy.

For those who prefer to unwind unaided by technological wizardry, home spa design also takes inspiration from the type of elemental bathing experience often encountered on holiday. Low- rather than high-tech, here the emphasis is on soothing, organic surroundings, a back-to-nature rather than back-to-the-future type of approach. Japanese hot tubs offer an unbeatable opportunity for soothing away stress with no gadgetry attached; overflow baths and sinks, such as the infinity-edge pool, rely on the gentle sound of trickling water for their calming effect. Steam rooms and saunas are time-honoured ways of delivering both deep cleansing and a profound sense of relaxation.

ABOVE LEFT The home spa puts the emphasis on relaxation. This wooden grid bridges a plunge pool. **ABOVE RIGHT** The bathroom as sybaritic retreat: home spas need not be high-tech, kitted out with the latest hydrotherapeutic gadgetry. Equally influential are more relaxed, organic environments. This example, with its large sunken pool and mattresses layered on the floor, is the perfect place to unwind. **RIGHT** A slatted-wood recliner, oval stone tub, and wood-burning stove create an environment for pampering the senses.

Siting and layout

This design approach usually demands plenty of floor area, both to accommodate fixtures and fittings and to provide essential breathing space. You can invest in the latest features, but then undermine their benefits if access to tubs or showers is awkward or if the room's layout is cramped and confined. If you do incorporate exercise machines, there should be enough room to position these at some remove from areas which are devoted purely to relaxation.

Technical specification will dictate where a home spa can be sited. Large Jacuzzis or whirlpool baths hold more water than a standard tub, which means that the floor must be strong enough to bear the weight. Other types of installation, such as steam rooms and saunas, require ancillary servicing. Most hydrotherapy baths and showers require high water pressure, assisted if necessary by a pump. Certain types of whirlpool bath need to be installed in such a way that the underside remains easily accessible.

Practicalities aside, the benefits of a home spa are greatly enhanced if it is located out of the general run of the household where you can relax in peace and quiet, free from distraction. An easy connection with the outdoors – at the very least a view and plenty of natural light – measurably adds to sensory enjoyment. A spa bath that is sunk in the floor or in a raised platform holds particular appeal. Many of the features of spa baths are specifically designed to simulate the sensation of lying in a natural whirlpool or rushing stream; a sunken bath helps to sustain this illusion.

ABOVE Here a sympathetic combination of stone and glass creates a clean-lined yet surprisingly tactile bathing environment. Special features include a rotating shower head and sunken whirlpool tub.

LEFT A bathtub is inset into a platform raised three steps from ground level, making good use of a fairly small area. The generous surround provides a handy surface for scented candles and other accessories that enhance relaxation.

Hydrotherapy

Hydrotherapy baths and showers aid relaxation and promote sensuous bliss. Manufacturers claim that therapeutic benefits can also be gained, including lower blood pressure, improved muscle tone, better circulation, greater mobility and clearer skin. By encouraging the release of lactic acid and other toxins from the body, stiff muscles and joints will be eased and the immune system strengthened, which is good news for those people with chronic back, muscular, or circulation problems. A great deal of research has gone into investigating the conditions for optimum relaxation. One manufacturer drew on NASA studies of weightlessness to determine that, when hips are at an angle of 135 degrees, stress on joints and muscles is reduced.

Different hydrotherapy systems are available, either individually or in combination. In a 'spa' bath, small jets at the bottom of the tub (200 jets in one particular top-flight model) release tiny bubbles of warmed air into the water for an effervescent 'champagne' effect that whispers across the skin, gently stimulating blood flow. In a whirlpool bath, jets of water have a stronger, more massaging effect. Roy Jacuzzi invented the whirlpool bath in 1964. The term 'Jacuzzi' has long since become generic, and there are many more manufacturers of this particular type of bath these days. In all whirlpool baths, a pump situated underneath pushes water through jets in the side of the bath, water which is then recirculated; in Jacuzzis, the water is mixed with air.

The degree of turbulence and strength of massage can be controlled – the trade literature terms 'whitewater' and 'rapids' give you some idea of the effects to be gained. The massaging effect is enhanced in larger baths because there is more room for the water to circulate. The number and position of jets are also important factors. Back jets may be rotating for deep massage, and jets may also be adjustable so that you can focus on a particular part of your body. Soft head- and armrests, which may or may not be removable, are also common options.

Special features include 'waterfalls' behind the headrest to massage the neck area, 'rainbow' cascades to fill the bathtub, underwater lighting, music systems, built-in heaters, descalers, and sanitizing systems. Top-of-the-range models use ultrasound to produce a deep, wave-like massage in combination with the water jets. A new development is a 'shiatsu' hydrotherapy bath, where four hydromassage jets are supplemented by 32 jets aligned with the body's pressure points. Combination spa and whirlpool baths are

also available. You can even convert standard or existing baths to spa or whirlpool baths. Remember, though, that installing the system is professional work.

As with most things, you get what you pay for. Cheaper whirlpools often pose a maintenance headache and can also be noisy, which undermines the whole point of the exercise.

Similar hydrotherapy features are available in showers. In this case, vertical and back jets (the strength of which can be controlled) deliver the massaging effect; shower heads can be adjusted to produce different types of spray, ranging from needle-fine to 'cloudburst'. Special features include rotary shower heads, cascades or waterfalls, integral seats, foot massage, and aromatherapy jets that disperse scented water.

Chromatherapy

Colour perception has psychological impact, as a result of the physical adjustments different wavelengths require from our eyes: green is considered the most calming colour because it requires little adjustment; red, which requires maximum adjustment, is arousing and stimulating. One of the latest bathing sensations on the market introduces coloured light to the spa experience. Both shower cubicles and baths can be fitted with LEDs so that the showerer or bather is washed by a succession of colours. The idea is that colour is a natural mood enhancer, with different hues stimulating different emotions. The effect can be enjoyed as a sequence or progression, or a particular colour can be chosen according to mood or preference. Advocates advise that different colours have different therapeutic properties. Violet, for example, is supposedly good at overcoming insomnia, while yellow is an antidepressant (banishes the blues, I suppose). I would, however, be a little concerned about someone who regularly bathed in red.

Steam rooms

In recent years, a steam room has become a sought-after feature in the upmarket bathroom. Steam bathing has an ancient history and well-known therapeutic properties. Wet heat opens the pores and produces perspiration, which flushes impurities from the skin and toxins from the system, increasing blood flow and enhancing skin tone. It is also recommended for those with chronic chest conditions as it eases constricted airways. Steam conducts heat better than air and can rise to very high temperatures – typically 40°–42°C (104°–106°F) with 100 per cent humidity. Pregnant women and those suffering from heart conditions should seek medical advice before taking a steam bath.

Hydrotherapy showers often include steam as one of their featured functions. Specially designed steam cabinets are also available. Shower enclosures can be converted into

FAR LEFT Hydrotherapy baths and showers are available in many different permutations. This marble-clad wet room features an overscaled 'rain' shower head and adjustable wall jets specially targeted to massage different areas of the body. **LEFT** Whirlpool baths simulate the effect of lying in a natural pool or stream; sunken tubs help to sustain the illusion even in an urban setting. **ABOVE** Chromatherapy is one of the latest developments in bathing technology. This chromatherapy bath by Kohler is fitted with LEDs which can be preset to a single colour or programmed to change colours in sequence. Proponents of chromatherapy ascribe different therapeutic powers to different shades.

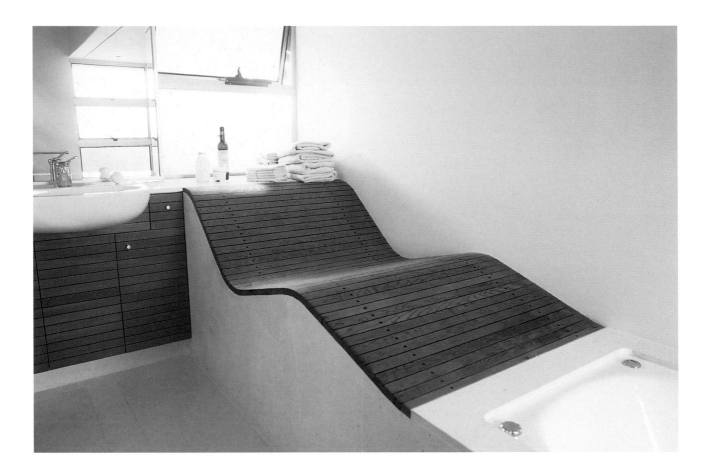

steam rooms relatively easily provided they are adequately sealed. Domes that fit over the top of the shower cubicle to keep steam in are available in a range of sizes. A steam generator, installed outside the enclosure, produces the steam; this is then delivered via a nozzle and controlled by a panel. The generator's power is set by the installer to suit the size of the room or enclosure. Built-in seats or benches make useful additions to the steam cabinet or enclosure, and it's an advantage to be able to recline.

A steam cabinet need not take up much room, and the generator itself can be sited in a vanity unit or cabinet, or even outside the bathroom. And it takes a mere 15 to 20 minutes to heat. As a bonus, steam softens bristles, which makes shaving easier. If you're going to shave in the steam, however, you'll need an electric demisting mirror.

Saunas

Bathing in dry heat also has a long history and is especially associated with Scandinavian countries. In general, saunas are hotter than steam baths, but the exceptionally low humidity (around 3 per cent) means that a sauna's high temperatures are easier to bear than you might think.

Saunas can be custom-built, or they are also available as ready-made cabins. The room should be well insulated and well ventilated. Walls are lined in untreated wood, often spruce, and air is heated by an electric or wood-burning stove. There are usually two levels of built-in wooden benches – the heat is greatest at the higher level.

Unlike steam cabinets, however, saunas cannot be considered particularly compact. Also, taking a sauna is a longer process than having a steam bath.

LEFT Reminiscent of Le Corbusier's famous bathroom at Villa Savoye, this home spa includes a built-in recliner for after-bath relaxation. The spa's undulating surface is faced in teak.

RIGHT Deep Japanese hot tubs are traditionally made of wood.

BELOW This steam and shower room has been built into an old coal cellar. Underfloor heating takes off the chill. A spout delivers steam into the room, while the steamer itself is located outside the cellar in an adjacent shed.

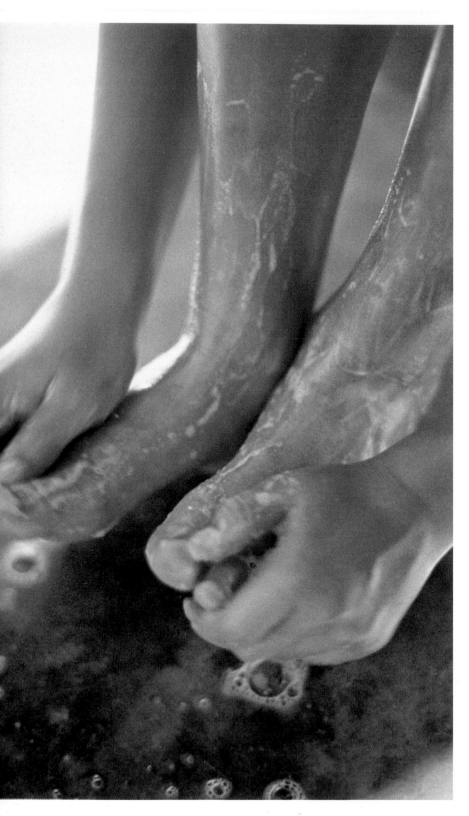

Hot tubs

Deep bathing in hot tubs is a gloriously uncomplicated way to relax. The Japanese hot tub is part of a bathing tradition whereby a long, often communal, soak is preceded by a cleansing shower. The tub is generally made of wood, which retains heat for a long time and has a pleasant woody smell. If the tub is covered with a lid overnight, the water will still be hot the next morning. Wooden tubs need to be kept filled with water between use or the wood will shrink and crack; even so, they generally require replacement after a period.

Overflow baths

Inspired by infinity edge pools, overflow baths create the sensation of floating in a rising tide. Water fills the bath to the brim, over which a gentle overflow cascades; for some people, the rhythmic sound of trickling water is inherently calming. Overflow baths are typically deep, which enhances the feeling of buoyancy; they are often mounted beneath a solid surround in a 'tub within a tub' effect. Inevitably, such features increase water consumption.

One unusual overflow design consists of an angled backrest made of Corian set within a glass box. Water spills over one end on to a pebble bed, from where it is drained.

Creating the environment

Whether you opt for the high- or low-tech route, the aim is the same: to create a restorative haven, a holistic milieu that appeals to all the senses and serves as an antidote to a stress-ridden modern lifestyle. Materials, decoration, and detail are critical factors when it comes to generating a peaceful, contemplative atmosphere.

Emphasize tactility by opting for natural materials for surfaces and finishes. Dimmable lights allow you to set levels high for exercising or working out, low for relaxing. Scent, candlelight, and soothing music – along with generous bathrobes and towels – add to the sybaritic experience.

RIGHT Overflow baths are the height of extravagance. Inspired by infinity-edge pools, these tubs are filled right to the brim, with the overflow cascading in a gentle trickle over the side. Designs are often of a 'tub within a tub' variety, and the depth of the water increases buoyancy.

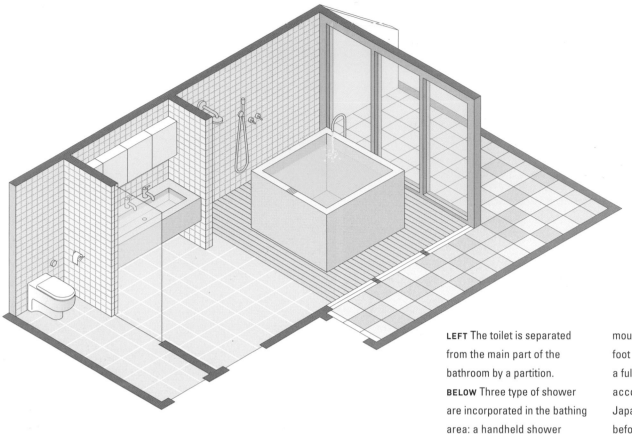

LEFT The toilet is separated from the main part of the bathroom by a partition.
BELOW Three type of shower are incorporated in the bathing area: a handheld shower mounted halfway up the wall, a foot shower in the corner, and a full-height shower head. This accords with the traditional Japanese practice of showering before soaking in a hot tub.

CASE STUDY **THE HOME SPA**

In this apartment, located on the top floor of a building in Stockholm, bathroom and adjoining roof terrace create a peaceful and private enclave, perfect for soaking away the stresses of modern life. Floor-to-ceiling windows that wrap around two sides of the bathing area, together with a sloping glass roof, flood the space with natural light and provide views of both the cityscape and the greenery on the terrace.

The focal point of the entire layout is a large Japanese-style soak tub, made of Swedish limestone; a full-height shower, foot shower, and handheld shower take care of basic cleansing. The tub is perfectly level; when full, water trickles in rivulets over grooves notched in the side and drains through the slatted teak floor to a concealed waste trap below. The only drawback is that, due to the fact that the apartment is on the top floor, water pressure is low and the tub takes some time to fill. Like the tub, the double sink in the adjoining area is made of Swedish limestone; at the far end, a toilet and small handbasin are screened behind a frosted-glass partition.

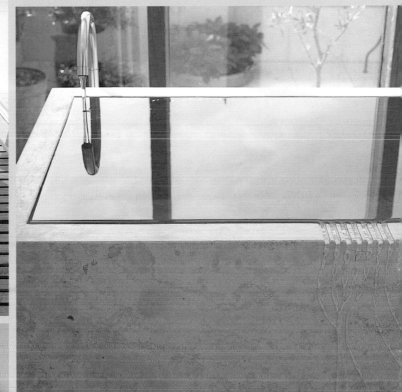

ABOVE LEFT AND ABOVE The large Swedish limestone tub has grooved channels in the side where water gently overflows. Sitting submerged in a great volume of water is inherently restful; the trickling sound of the overflow provides a soothing accompaniment. **LEFT** The walls are tiled in white ceramic. Above the limestone double basin are mirrored cabinets which reflect the light. The large shower head is by Boffi; the taps (faucets) are Vola.

LEFT In hot climates and in seaside areas, outdoor bathing can be irresistible. This house in the Caribbean has an outdoor deck complete with wall-mounted sink and outdoor shower, well screened by tropical vegetation for privacy.

RIGHT Even in more temperate parts of the world, the sensation of bathing outdoors can be enhanced by making the most of views and natural light, as is the case in this environmentally friendly 'solar tube' house with its bowed transparent cladding.

INDOOR/OUTDOOR

The elemental pleasure of water on skin is heightened outdoors; the feeling of being part of the natural world engages all of the senses.

In pursuit of such basic enjoyment, people from less temperate climates fly hundreds of miles at considerable expense to holiday beside the sea in warm climates – or stay at home and spend even more money installing a swimming pool in their back garden. Even those of us who do benefit from living in a sunny climate can sometimes forget the sheer pleasure of bathing outdoors. Yet this is a sensory experience that need not be overlooked because you live somewhere cool and rainy, nor taken for granted because every summer is an almost endless succession of hot, sunny skies.

Contact with nature – the sun, a fresh breeze, the sky overhead – does not have to be restricted to the annual two weeks' break nor to those wealthy enough to afford a pool. If the walls are definitely coming down around the bathroom inside the home, the boundaries between indoors and outdoors are clearly also being dissolved.

The irresistible appeal of outdoor bathing is all too easy to gauge. Even in urban areas, where nature is often at one remove, and in parts of the world where the weather is not consistently reliable, people are increasingly taking the opportunity to build this type of experience into daily life. One well-publicized example was the shower fashion designer Stella McCartney installed on the roof of her West London home. Showering under a night sky or even under a gentle London rain restores a natural dimension to hectic city life.

If such a degree of exposure is not for you, there are still ways in which nature in the form of sunlight, fresh air, and greenery can be brought closer to home. In Japan, where space is at a premium, there is an understanding of the central role of nature in our lives. Traditionally, every room or space in the home must contain at least one living reminder of the natural world, even if this is no more than a single bloom.

Light and air

Making sure that bathing areas have maximum natural light and are well ventilated with fresh air can go a long way towards creating a more natural environment. If you have the choice, consider siting the bathroom so that it benefits from good light conditions at the time you use it most regularly. An east-facing orientation will give good natural light at the beginning of the day; south-facing (in the northern hemisphere), north-facing (in the southern hemisphere), or west-facing locations mean plenty of warming sunshine in the afternoon and early evening – although west-facing may not be a good choice in a particularly hot, sunny climate.

Expanses of glazing and windows or external doors which can be fully opened bring in light and allow air to circulate. If privacy is an issue, but you don't want to block light unnecessarily, you could glaze the lower portions of windows or openings with frosted or etched glass, or infill openings with glass blocks or bricks which admit the light but obscure views. Windows or openings on opposite walls encourage cooling through breezes to circulate, stirring up the air in a refreshing and invigorating way.

Where extensive glazing would result in excess heat loss in winter, you might consider choosing low-E glass which keeps heat in. Where bathrooms are otherwise internal or are sited in areas where natural light is poor, toplighting in the form of skylights is very effective. There's something utterly appealing about lying in the bath and gazing at a patch of clear, blue sky or the night stars. Skylights that can open allow warm, humid air to escape.

In hot climates where the light is strong, some form of screening will be necessary to prevent the bathroom overheating through passive solar gain. Slatted blinds, wooden louvres, slatted shutters, and pierced screens create evocative patterns of light and shade, while allowing air to circulate through open windows.

TOP LEFT Here, a slatted ceiling creates moody bands of light and shade in a timber-clad shower area. **LEFT** A pivoting glass door separates a Shinto-inspired shower, with the shower head installed in the ceiling, from a secluded terrace where bathers can dry off in the heat of the Australian sun. **ABOVE** A suspended panel partially encloses a shower area without blocking light or panoramic views.

Dissolving the boundaries

The closest connections with nature can be forged either at ground level or on the rooftop, locations which offer the possibility of full exposure to the outdoors. Bathing areas that immediately adjoin gardens or are sited so they are partially exposed are nothing new. Roman baths typically incorporated garden areas, as did the traditional Japanese bathhouse. As with en suite arrangements, the connection between the two areas is underscored if they are designed to be complementary. Using similar materials indoors and out – for example, wooden flooring meeting wooden decking, or stone tiling meeting stone paviours – helps to blur the boundaries between the two. In reliably warm climates, you can arrange matters so that the wall separating an indoor bathing area from the garden opens up fully to take advantage of cooling breezes and views. Where the climate is less hospitable, extensive glazing, sliding screens, or French doors maintain a visual connection with outdoor areas while keeping the weather out.

ABOVE A bath with a view … wraparound windows provide a stunning panorama of a desert landscape.

LEFT An up-and-over door rises to unite the bathroom with the outdoors. The freestanding tub is a Starck design. The terrace immediately adjoining the bathroom is shaded from strong sunlight by latticed timberwork.

RIGHT Alternate panels of clear and frosted glass allow light to stream through while preserving an element of privacy.

LEFT Who actually needs a
shower curtain when you are
able to shower outdoors?
BELOW This Australian outdoor
shower comprises a floor made
of river stone, corrugated-iron walls, and a zinc door. It is
shaded by native trees.
RIGHT Simple slatted timber
panels framed in metal provide
minimal screening for an outdoor shower and wash area.

While bathrooms are less exclusively private places than they were some years ago, and while we may now be comfortable with the idea of sharing a bath with close family or friends, that does not necessarily mean that privacy is no longer an issue. Bathing areas that open out into gardens run the risk of being overlooked. Even if you are happy to bare all, your neighbours may not share the same relaxed attitude to alfresco bathing and could take offence. Screening an outdoor bathing area – or an indoor but visible one – with trellis, fencing, or planting, or a combination of the three, will provide the necessary shield from prying eyes. Luxuriant ferns and bamboos make a living backdrop to an outdoor tub or pool. Unless you want to trip down the garden seminaked, position an outdoor shower or tub where there is easy access to indoors.

An elevated terrace or roof garden is another potential site for an outdoor bathing area. Stella McCartney's outdoor shower formed part of a roof terrace surrounded by 1.8-m (6-ft) wooden fencing. Again, privacy and overlooking are issues to be addressed, as are more practical structural concerns. A roof terrace that can support a few containerized plants may not be strong enough to bear the weight of a filled bath: check conditions with a structural engineer. Showers and baths must be adequately drained, with the surrounding areas fully waterproofed to prevent water lying on the surface and creating a potential risk of damp penetration to the underlying roof structure. There may also be planning issues: Stella's outdoor shower only became newsworthy because of complaints from neighbours, who objected not to the presence of the shower, but to the fencing that screened the terrace. Be sure to seek advice from local planning authorities on whether what you intend to construct is within the bounds of permitted development.

Showers and tubs

Judicious choice of fixtures and fittings can restore an instinctive simplicity to the daily rituals of bathing and washing. Minimalism, which takes inspiration from Zen Buddhism, results in a pared-down environment where there is little to intervene between you and nature's basic elements of light, air, and space.

Showers in the form of simple spouts or angled upright pipes, traditional Japanese hot tubs, and overflow baths and sinks are in keeping with this spare aesthetic. Like overflow baths, so-called 'wet surface' sinks exploit the calming effect of flowing water. Here, water falls into a shallow dish and overflows on to a flat surface, draining away via a grooved channel around the perimeter. 'Rain' showers feature overscaled heads which provide a bigger shower area and can be controlled to produce anything from gentle spring rain to a tropical downpour.

Hot tubs and Jacuzzis sited on outdoor decks were once considered synonymous with a laid-back West Coast lifestyle; today, they have even spread to countries such as Britain, where the weather is less reliable than sunny southern California and where hedonism has not typically been anything approaching a national trait.

Spa and whirlpool baths can be sited outdoors, but their aesthetic appeal often leaves much to be desired. By contrast, wooden hot tubs, whether freestanding or sunk in decking, are more visually compatible with garden locations. Wooden tubs have integral bench seating so you can sit fully submerged up to your neck in water; they are available with similar jet-massage features to those of spa baths. These require professional installation to establish the necessary electrical connections, but they can be filled with a garden hose if you would rather not extend plumbing outdoors. If the tub is kept on an economy setting and fully covered when not in use, the water will remain warm and will heat up to bathing temperature quickly when required; running costs are not astronomical. Some manufacturers of hot tubs also supply gazebos to provide an enclosure for the tub – a boon in either inclement or scorchingly hot weather.

FAR LEFT Here is an indoor shower with an outdoor feel. Its walls are polished concrete, painted a soft charcoal colour, while the roof is glass. The choice of minimal fixtures, including an overscaled shower head, helps to create a mood of natural simplicity.
LEFT This mosaic-tiled wet room gives on to a decked sun terrace for easy connection between indoors and outdoors.
BELOW A guesthouse in the Netherlands features an outdoor spa area, complete with a Finnish red cedar soak tub and Boffi shower.

Creating the environment

As with the home spa approach, natural surfaces and materials, considered in tandem with those employed in adjoining outdoor areas, help to perpetuate the mood of tranquil contemplation. Dynamic artificial lighting adds to the effect. Hot tubs with integral fibre-optic lighting create glowing outdoor focal points. Fibre-optics can also be used to light running water from taps (faucets) or shower basins.

Greenery is always a bonus. Tropical and semitropical plants such as tree ferns flourish in the warm, humid atmosphere created by a bathroom. Outdoors, scented plants such as lavender and rosemary provide living aromatherapy when planted near a hot tub.

LEFT A view of the bathroom from the raised gravel bed. In keeping with the Japanese aesthetic, the exterior of the extension is clad in cedar, a water-resistant wood traditionally used to construct Japanese hot tubs and which needs no weatherproofing.
RIGHT The cast-iron rolltop bath sits on hunks of iroko. The spout comes up from the floor; taps (faucets) are mounted on one of the iroko blocks. Skylights and extensive glazing bathe the space in natural light. Flooring is white ceramic mosaic tile.

CASE STUDY **INDOOR/OUTDOOR**

The rituals associated with traditional Japanese bathing were the point of reference for this design in south London. The clients' brief to the architect was to create a bathroom that reflected an Eastern sensibility and which had the strongest possible connection with the garden. Accordingly, it was sited at ground level in a purpose-built extension that forms the culmination of a sequence of progression from interior to exterior.

In most homes, bathrooms are directly accessible from other interior areas. Here, the bathroom extension is linked to the house by a covered side passage with a glazed roof and large glazed window, so the effect is almost one of walking through the garden to reach the bathroom. The best view of the garden in the whole house is from the bathtub, which is positioned at one end of the extension in front of a big window. As most of the garden is lower down, the outside area immediately adjoining the bathroom is a raised gravel bed, with bamboo planted at the far end screening views from neighbours.

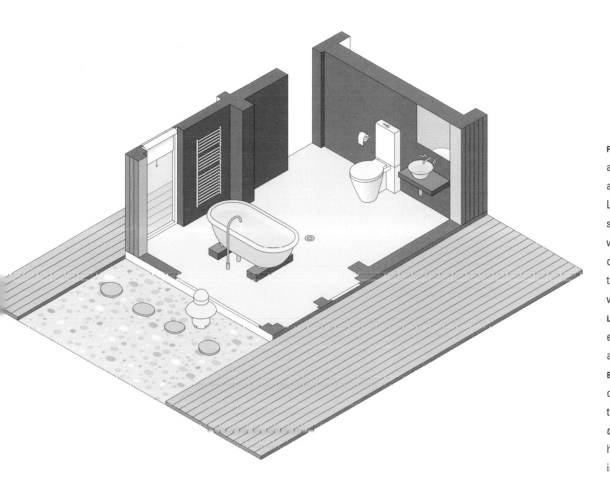

FAR LEFT The walls and ceilings are covered in plywood, stained almost black and lacquered. Light reflected off near-black surfaces is very defined and white. The effect is to make changing light values at different times of the day and in different weather much more evident.

LEFT The bathroom forms an extension to the main house, accessed via a glazed passage.

BELOW The toilet and white ceramic bowl mounted on a thick slab of iroko are aligned along one wall. The shower head, seen reflected in a mirror, is fixed to a ceiling beam.

For much of the twentieth century, the design of what the trade terms 'sanitaryware' remained remarkably static. The chief variable was colour: think 'avocado bathroom suite' and you are immediately transported to the late 1960s. Although acrylic bathtubs were first introduced in the 1970s, a development which made new shapes possible, most sinks and toilets were still made in glazed ceramic and in standardized designs and sizes.

Today, if bathrooms have become bigger and more inclusive, fixtures and fittings have also undergone dramatic change. Mass retailers supply sanitaryware in a variety of materials unthinkable a decade or so ago, everything from glass to steel, wood to stone. At the top end are custom-made tubs and sinks, carved in marble, stone, or wood, or cast in concrete, and innovative, sculptural ranges created by leading architects and designers such as Philippe Starck, Mark Newson, Norman Foster, David Chipperfield, Claudio Silvestrin, Antonio Citterio – and even Conran! To complement these, a wealth of fixtures is available, varying as widely in function and performance as they do in aesthetics and design.

Breadth of choice brings freedom of expression, but it does complicate the decision-making process somewhat. Bearing in mind that a 'fixture' is truly that – something that is permanently installed – and that upmarket models may entail considerable outlay, you need to be certain that your selection will suit your personal needs and preferences, both now and in the future.

When it comes to colour, white still dominates the market. Aside from the obvious associations with freshness and hygiene, white is often the more practical choice. If you opt for a coloured suite and then need to replace a single item at a later date, precise colour matching can be problematic.

BATHROOM FIXTURES

BATHTUBS

The bathtub is the most dominant fixture in the bathroom, not merely by virtue of its size, but also because bathing takes more time than other bathroom activities. A bath that isn't comfortable or doesn't fit your frame particularly well obviously represents a major shortfall in basic practicality.

Although coordination of design across all the fixtures that comprise a suite is generally a good idea, particularly in a small bathroom where cohesion is vital, the bathtub is one element which can be selected on an individual basis, in terms of both material and form. Devotees of the traditional cast-iron bathtub or aficionados of the latest sculptural tub can combine such features with toilets and sinks that display a different aesthetic without detracting unduly from the overall result. A bath can even become a centrepiece.

Choosing a bathtub

There are a number of practical considerations which should inform your choice. Don't be shy about trying out a bath before you buy it – what is comfortable when you are dry and fully clothed is bound to be even more comfortable when you're immersed in water. Lean your head back to make sure there is adequate support for your neck. Tubs that are too long can be just as uncomfortable as those which are too short; most people like to brace their feet against the end of the bath.

Size and shape The bottom line is that the bathtub should fit both your physical frame and the space at your disposal. Can you stretch out fully in the tub? Would a corner or asymmetric bathtub make better use of existing floor space than a standard model? Think about who will be using the bathtub in the main. Double-ended shapes allow two people to bathe in comfort, while bathtubs with contoured or reclining interiors limit you to more or less one position, which may not suit your needs.

FAR LEFT Bathtubs are available in a wide range of shapes, styles and materials. Many contemporary designs are made of acrylic. This modern tub has a pop-up waste; wall-mounted taps (faucets) and a handheld shower attachment keep the immediate area surrounding the bath clear. **LEFT** Cast-iron baths are still produced in limited quantities today; if you cannot find a new one, secondhand reconditioned examples are widely available from salvage yards and similar outlets. Typical features of the cast-iron tub include a rolltop edge and decorative claw feet.

Depth Is the bathtub deep enough for total immersion? Tubs that are very deep, on the other hand, may be awkward if you like to read in the bath, if you are bathing small children, or if you have restricted mobility. American bathtubs are generally shallower than European and British versions.

Weight Heavy bathtubs, particularly those made of cast iron or stone, can impose additional loads on the floor structure and so may not be suitable. Lighter tubs, such as those made from acrylic, are easier to install. Acrylic may be the only practical choice if you want a large tub, given the additional weight of the water that you need to factor in when considering whether the floor is strong enough to support it.

Warmth Certain materials retain heat better than others. Acrylic and wood keep water warm for longer than stone or concrete, which also take a long time to heat up. This consideration becomes more critical the larger the bathtub, as water may cool faster than you can fill the tub.

Maintenance How easy is the bathtub to clean? How resilient is it to superficial scratching and cracking? Are there particular maintenance requirements? Wooden tubs, for example, need to be kept filled between use or they are prone to shrinkage and cracking.

Water consumption Very large or very deep baths consume more water than standard models, as do overflow or infinity-edge models. The bigger the bath, the longer it will take to fill. You should consider not only the likely cost and practicality of using a lot of water, but also the environmental factors. Water is a precious resource, particularly in some climates, and should never be wasted.

Function Will you require additional facilities, such as an overbath shower, an integral hand shower, or perhaps hydrotherapy functions? Does the bathtub come with tap (faucet) holes already drilled, or do you have a choice when it comes to where fixtures can be mounted?

Cast iron

Cast-iron bathtubs were first mass-manufactured in the early decades of the twentieth century, and they remain a popular choice today, particularly at the luxury end of the market. The manufacturing process is complicated and time consuming: one bathtub can take several days to produce. Several layers of porcelain enamel are fused on to a cast-iron shell to provide a white, glossy, smooth surface. A slight unevenness of finish is part of the appeal. There are few remaining manufacturers; most cast-iron baths are now made in Portugal and Spain.

Cast-iron baths are extremely durable, being highly scratchproof and crackproof, and resistant to staining. They have a nice, substantial feel and good heat-insulating qualities, although they may feel chilly to begin with. These baths are heavy, however, which can cause problems with installation, and they are expensive.

Shapes tend to be conventional, owing to the constraints imposed by the manufacturing process and the material itself. Single- or double-ended versions are available, as well as slipper bathtubs, which are shorter and have a raised back. Freestanding bathtubs typically come with a rolltop edge and the option of decorative claw feet in brass, chrome, or cast iron; they may also be supported in a number of other

ways, including shaped wooden blocks. The cast-iron exterior may be black or supplied unfinished for decorative painting. Cast-iron bathtubs with flat tops suitable for setting under solid surfaces are also available.

Cast-iron bathtubs can be obtained secondhand from salvage yards and similar outlets. If the finish is worn, stained or pitted, the bath will need respraying, reconditioning or re-enamelling; the most effective repair jobs are the most expensive. You should also check that tap (faucet) holes are sized and positioned to suit your requirements. If you have acquired a cast-iron bathtub along with a recently purchased house, respraying can be carried out in situ.

Steel

In pressed-steel bathtubs, the enamelling is done on a steel base. These are much cheaper and lighter than cast-iron bathtubs. They come in a wide variety of shapes and sizes, with integral panels (or aprons), and in a full range of colours. Edges may be rounded, thick or standard. Types include freestanding rolltop bathtubs, those designed to be inset or enclosed by panelling, and shower baths which have flat bases and are wider at the shower end. Pressed-steel bathtubs are not as durable as cast-iron ones. They are also noisier and do not retain heat well. A further disadvantage is that they are very slippery.

Stainless-steel bathtubs have a robust, industrial aesthetic. Some retailers supply freestanding stainless-steel baths that are handmade to individual specification.

ABOVE New cast-iron baths often come without tap (faucet) holes, which gives greater freedom for positioning the taps. This slipper bath has taps mounted centrally. All cast-iron bathtubs are heavy, so you need to check that the existing floor structure can bear the strain of the additional load.

ABOVE RIGHT Acrylic is light, which means larger sizes are feasible; it can also be fashioned into a wide range of shapes. This freestanding acrylic bath comes from Starck's Edition 2 range. **RIGHT** A vibrant red bath and matching trough sink made of Durat, a composite material.

Acrylic

Acrylic bathtubs vary widely in quality and price. The best are reinforced with fibreglass and have an underlying support structure to enhance rigidity and improve insulation. When first introduced, acrylic bathtubs were regarded as a substandard substitute, but that is far from the case today.

Acrylic is very light and can be precisely detailed, which means that a wide variety of shapes and sizes is possible. Because the material is so light, bathtubs can be much larger than those made in heavy materials such as cast iron. A huge range of colours is available, as well as semimatt finishes. Types include freestanding bathtubs, such as the Starck Edition 2, corner and offset designs, circular bathtubs, and bathtubs with contoured interiors.

ABOVE The ultimate in bathing luxury is a carved stone bathtub. All stone tubs, whether they are limestone or marble, are exceedingly heavy and very expensive. ABOVE RIGHT Pressed-steel and acrylic baths are commonly inset under surrounds and enclosed by panelling. In this example, both cladding and surround are made of wood. ABOVE FAR RIGHT Wooden bathtubs are warm and silky smooth. This 'Woodline' tub by Agape is made of marine ply, which is highly water-resistant, and incorporates moulded seating.

Unlike cast-iron or steel bathtubs, the enamelled surface of which will always have imperfections, no matter how minute, acrylic is a homogenous material. Scratches or other superficial damage can be easily restored; a bathtub that has dulled to matt can be brought up to a shine with fine metal polish. Acrylic bathtubs are much more hygienic than other types and are easy to clean, warm, and non-slip.

A similar composite material, Durat, is made of 50 per cent recycled plastics. It can be cut and shaped with woodworking tools and jointed with special glue. Although the material is more commonly used to make sinks and surrounds, it can also be used to construct bathtubs. Durat has a silky texture and is extremely durable, easy to maintain, and warm. A range of colours is available to choose from, in a typically speckled finish.

Stone

Bathtubs made of stone or artificial stone have a certain patrician, indeed monumental, quality. The most expensive – and the heaviest – are carved from solid blocks of limestone or marble. One particular example designed by Claudio Silvestrin, a carved limestone tub in the form of a circular bowl, weighs as much as a Volkswagen Golf – and it doesn't cost much less, either. Cheaper and lighter are bathtubs that are made from stone panels or slabs jointed and reinforced at the corners. Cheaper still are those made of artificial stone. While such bathtubs may have a beautiful sculptural presence, remember that stone is a chilly material and thus bathwater will not stay warm for long.

Wood

Wooden bathtubs gained in popularity with the vogue for minimalist decor. The reference point is the traditional Japanese soaking tub, which is deeper and shorter than Western equivalents, so that the bather sits immersed to chin level. Both off-the-peg and bespoke versions are available. Non-resinous, naturally waterproof wood, such as cedar and teak, as well as chestnut, Japanese cypress, and black pine, is suitable; some species even have an attractive scent. If wood is your choice of material, the tub itself must be carefully constructed so that all the joints are tight-fitting. Even so, it is still advisable to keep wooden bathtubs filled between soaks so that the wood does not dry out, leading to shrinkage and splits. A bonus is that wood has such high insulating properties that a lid placed over the tub will keep water warm until the next day.

Wooden bathtubs will not last for ever, though, and eventually need to be replaced. If you do opt for a wooden bathtub, you should adopt the Japanese practice of showering first so that you do not soak in dirty water.

Concrete and tile

Concrete tubs can be cast in situ by a specialist contractor or constructed in a wooden formwork. As with stone, weight is a significant factor when deciding whether concrete is a suitable choice. Concrete bathtubs are generally finished in waterproof plaster or render of the type used in swimming pools. Other types of cladding include mosaic tile.

Glass

Glass sinks or 'vessels' are increasingly common, even in mass-market outlets, but glass bathtubs remain a rather more exclusive preserve. Whatever form it takes, a glass tub is undoubtedly a showstopper and a focal point, the transparency of the material making an evocative match with water. Most glass bathtubs are custom-designed and made from toughened glass, similar to that employed to make observation panels in aquaria and swimming pools. Structural sealant between the joints permits frameless construction and minimal detailing.

Special features

A wide range of spa-type bathtubs is available, from Jacuzzis and whirlpools to chromatherapy baths which wash you in colour as well as water (see page 111). Hydrotherapy features can also be fitted to standard bathtubs. Another recent development is the overflow bathtub, often designed in the form of a tub within a tub, where water cascades over the edge and is drained away from the base (page 114).

ABOVE The cutting edge of design: an overflow bath made of tempered glass with an inclined Corian base. Water spills over the end into a pebble bed from where it is drained to a floor waste. TOP A custom-made square bathtub tiled in black mosaic overlooks a water garden. At night, with the lights dimmed, the boundaries of the tub seem to disappear. RIGHT If the floor is strong enough a specialist contractor can cast a concrete shower tray or bath in situ. This rough-cast example is fitted with a suitably utilitarian shower head.

FAR LEFT A wall-hung ceramic sink in the form of a trough is large enough for two people to wash at the same time, something which helps to avoid those peak-time traffic jams if yours is a busy household.
LEFT Glass sinks possess an undeniable glamour and sense of drama. Here, a backlit plinth turns a simple glass tank into a glowing focal point.
RIGHT Reclaimed sinks have retro appeal. This enamelled steel sink is fitted with a pair of period taps (faucets).

SINKS

Choosing a bathroom sink is undoubtedly a more involved affair than it was in the days when the biggest variable was colour. Today, sinks are available in every shape and size, in materials ranging from glass to wood, and in a host of sculptural forms. But while the sink as 'design statement' has definitely arrived, it is still important to pay attention to practicalities of maintenance and durability, as well as use.

Function is an important consideration, and there are more variables than might at first appear. Do you wash your hands under running water, or do you like to put in the plug and fill the sink? Will someone who shaves be using the sink? Do you use the sink for handwashing delicate articles of clothing? Does it need to be big enough for two people to access it at the same time, or would a pair of sinks be better? A sink in a master or shared bathroom is used more frequently than one in a cloakroom or guest bathroom, which means it should be easy to keep in pristine condition.

Size can be misleading. A 'vessel' or sink that sits on top of a surface or vanity unit may appear smaller than a sink with an integral surround, but may be comparable in terms of actual washing area or volume of water. Small sinks are space saving, but you run the risk of soaking the floor or adjacent areas if you intend using them for more than simply washing your hands.

Height is another variable. While pedestal sinks commit you to a standard height, other types allow you to position the sink at the level which is most comfortable. Bear in mind, however, that wall-hung sinks must be either mounted on a solid or load-bearing wall, or supported by brackets.

Aside from vessel-type sinks, most sinks come already drilled with tap (faucet) holes. Some will have a single tap hole only, for a mixer tap; others will have three tap holes for the faucet and the hot and cold taps; and others still are available with either option.

Types of sink

One of the most familiar types of sink is that designed to be inset into a countertop or built in within a vanity unit. These come in a range of shapes and sizes, and make good practical sense in a bathroom where storage is a key requirement. Inset or semi-inset sinks can be fixed at any height. An inset sink is designed to be dropped into a surround or vanity top, with only the top edge proud of the surface; in the case of a semi-inset sink, the front of the sink projects slightly from the vanity unit. Even neater are underbowls which are fixed directly underneath a vanity top or surround. The top edge of an underbowl is unglazed so that the sink can be stuck in place with a watertight join. Undermounting provides a seamless finish and means that there are no awkward edges that are difficult to clean.

Another standard type is the pedestal sink, where the pedestal is either a separate element or part of a monoblock design. Because the pedestal, which is designed to conceal pipework, is such an obvious feature, it is advisable to choose a toilet that matches. Pedestals come in a range of styles from contemporary to retro, but a disadvantage is that the sink will be set at a standard height, generally between 850 and 900mm (34 and 36in).

More flexible in terms of positioning are half-pedestal sinks with siphon covers. Siphon covers conceal pipework, but do not extend to the floor. Instead, they are fitted to the sink or wall, or both. Small hand basins and corner sinks without either pedestals or siphon covers should be fitted with a 'bottle trap', which is a metal waste in a finish that matches the taps (faucets). Such designs are particularly suited to small bathrooms or any situation where you want to keep the floor area clear.

The newest and most innovative sink designs ironically hark back to the days of bedroom washstands when the 'sink' comprised a china bowl and jug of water. These freestanding basins – termed 'vessels' or 'lavatories' in North America – have grown in popularity ever since 1995 when

ABOVE A pair of sinks set into matching wooden vanity units has a neat, furnished look. The units conceal plumbing while providing storage space.
LEFT Claudio Silvestrin's carved stone sink mounted into a stone edge is an elegant play on the geometries of sphere and plane.
RIGHT Starck's first bathroom range, Edition 1, includes this sink set in a cylindrical pear-wood unit. The inspiration for the design was the basic form of a bucket.

Philippe Starck designed a version for the Delano Hotel in Miami. 'Vessel' sinks have a centre hole for drainage and are either poised on a counter or another similar surface, or suspended from a wall-mounted bracket. Taps generally have to be fitted behind or on the wall above and need to be long enough and high enough to reach the bowl; they must also be accurately positioned so that water drains directly to the waste, otherwise there will be the risk of splashing. Vessel sinks do not have overflows, so they must be fitted with a grid drain.

The appeal of these designs is largely owing to their sculptural quality and the range of evocative, tactile materials in which they are made. At the same time, because they are so minimal, freestanding sinks have the effect of making a room look larger; as they sit higher than standard sinks, they also minimize bending and splashing on the part of their user. For a more furnished look, vessel sinks can be fitted into the top drawer of a chest or mounted on a table.

Wet surface or 'wet table' sinks are another recent development. Here, as in the case of the overflow bathtub, water runs off a wet surface and is drained around the perimeter. One particular model comes with a separate bowl with a hole in the base; the bowl sits on the wet surface to collect water while you are washing and then can be lifted clear. Wet tables, with their constant trickle of running water, are designed to create the soothing effect of an indoor fountain; they are rather wasteful in terms of water consumption.

Again, as with baths, sinks can be commissioned from specialist contractors or suppliers, and designed to individual size and specification, which can be a good way of obtaining a sink in an unusual material, size, or shape. For instance, shallow water troughs that run the length of a wall and are fitted with several individual taps can provide a neater solution to shared facilities than double basins.

Reclaimed sinks and basins are also available from specialist outlets and salvage yards should you wish to choose this route for something a little different. Choice varies between retro-style sinks that might once have graced the bathrooms of grand hotels to utilitarian metal troughs and basins from laboratories or hospitals, which have a more overtly industrial aesthetic. If tap holes and wastes are not compatible with the design of modern fixtures, you will need to acquire period or specialist fixtures as well.

Materials and maintenance

Despite recent trends, most sinks are still made of ceramic or vitreous china, a material which has obvious practical advantages. Although not durable enough for the type of punishment a kitchen sink would endure, ceramic bathroom sinks will stand up perfectly well to years of normal use without chipping and are hygienic and easy to clean. A ceramic sink will, however, irreparably crack or chip if you drop a heavy object on it. The range of colours available is vast; if colour matching to decor is crucial, it is important to view a real sample in context. Colour matching within ranges is generally not problematic, but variations in manufacturing mean that differences are bound to show up if you mix a sink from one range with a toilet from another.

Sinks made of glass, stone, glazed terracotta, steel, copper, and wood undoubtedly offer the shock of the new. When combined with accent lighting from above or below, they create dramatic focal points. A sink made of an unusual material may introduce a tactile element into the design equation, but there are certain implications in terms of maintenance and durability.

The best glass sinks are finished with a fired-on silicone coating which makes them easier to keep clean. Otherwise, glass sinks are probably not best suited to heavy use. Stone sinks or vessels have an appealing tactility, but in conditions of extreme heat – for example, if you use the sinks for steam treatments – there may be the risk of cracking. Stainless steel is virtually damage-proof, resisting scratches, staining, and chipping, which is why such fixtures are often specified for utility applications such as washrooms in hospitals and prisons. Water- and toothpaste-spotting can, however, be an issue. The easiest to maintain have a brushed, matt finish. Wooden sinks are often made of marine ply, stained to look like oak, teak, or wenge, but a real teak sink is practical and good to use.

FAR LEFT Some glass vessel sinks have a surface coating which repels water. Taps (faucets) must be long enough to direct water straight to the centre drain in order to prevent splashing. **ABOVE LEFT** Many wooden sinks are made of marine ply. Teak is another naturally water-resistant wood. **ABOVE** Sinks have now become a design statement. This ceramic sink was designed by Mark Newson for Ideal Standard. **ABOVE RIGHT** A stainless-steel sink in the form of a shallow trough is reminiscent of the type of fixtures found in a laboratory setting.

TOILETS & BIDETS

Ever since Nancy Mitford wrote her acerbic guide to manners, the term 'lavatory' has been widely regarded as socially acceptable, or 'U', whereas 'toilet' has most definitely been 'non-U'. That is, in Britain at least. In North America, a 'lavatory' is a sink. Nevertheless, on both sides of the linguistic divide, this essential fixture is more usually known by any one of a number of colloquialisms, from the humorous to the more euphemistically genteel, which says a great deal about the coyness with which we still approach basic bodily functions.

Terminology aside, the toilet – or WC unit, in architectural parlance – is the most complicated of all bathroom fixtures and, until fairly recently, has been the most conservative in design. While flushing systems for toilets have seen various modifications and improvements over the years, appearance and style have been slow to change. Adamsez made the breakthrough in the late 1960s and still produces some of the most elegant toilets and bidets around. Philippe Starck, too, has been a pioneer in this respect and, following the launch of his early bathroom range – where the lavatory took the elemental form of a pail or bucket – other designers have followed suit. Today, toilets and bidets are designed with as much attention to sculptural form as baths and sinks.

Because the toilet must be connected directly to the soil stack, options for positioning may be fairly restricted. This, in turn, may have a bearing on the type of toilet you choose.

Flushing systems

To flush a toilet, a volume of water must be discharged into the pan at sufficient pressure. There are two principal ways that this is achieved. In Britain, cisterns contain a siphon or U-shaped pipe. When the toilet is flushed, usually with a lever handle, the siphon is opened and atmospheric pressure forces water up the pipe and down into the toilet. The siphon system, which was invented in the nineteenth century, was designed to prevent leaks. The disadvantage of the system, however, is that the first litre (¼ US gallon) of water drawn up by the siphon does not reach the bowl with sufficient pressure to flush the toilet. It is the 6.5 litres (1¾ US gallons) or so that follow that do the job.

Elsewhere around the world, WCs employ valve flush mechanisms. When the toilet is flushed, often by means of a push button at the top of the cistern, the valve inside the cistern is pulled up, releasing a flow of water directly into the toilet bowl. This immediate water pressure means that less water is needed to flush the toilet and that the flush itself is faster, in some German models twice the rate of a siphon system. Flushes are also quieter and cisterns can be more compact because they do not have to hold so much water.

Until recently, valve flush mechanisms were banned in Britain because they were prone to leakage. Following changes to legislation which came into effect in 2001, valves can now be used instead of siphons, provided their design is officially approved. Push-button toilet conversion kits incorporating flapper valves are available for adapting existing cisterns. There are also dual-flush valve systems on the market, which offer the option of a low 3-litre (US ¾-gallon) flush to conserve water, as well as the normal full flush.

Water consumption

With increased need for water conservation, a need which is only likely to increase in the future, legislation in different parts of the world now governs the volume of flush. The previous flush volume of 7.5 litres (2 US gallons) has now been reduced to 6 litres (about 1⅔ US gallons) in Britain,

RIGHT Wall-hung toilets, where the cistern is concealed behind a panel or false wall, are neat and discreet. Here, a shelf recessed into the false wall behind the toilet provides a convenient place to store a few paperbacks.

LEFT This decorative restored Victorian lavatory with high-level cistern and solid wood seat is a good illustration of the reason why 'throne' is a popular slang term for toilet.

RIGHT Very much the smallest room, this toilet is sited in what amounts to a cupboard, hidden behind antique wooden doors.

BELOW A floor-mounted toilet with a concealed cistern and push-button flush is separated from the rest of the bathroom by a glass screen.

Europe and the United States, and looks likely to fall further, perhaps as low as 4.5 litres (1⅛ US gallons). Legislation applies not to existing fixtures, but to new installations. Low-flush toilets used to be very inefficient, which meant people flushed them twice, in the end saving little water at all. New models, however, are much improved.

Components of the toilet

The two basic components of the toilet are the cistern or tank, and the toilet pan or bowl. Fewer exposed parts and fewer connections mean that the toilet is less obtrusive and easier to keep clean. Traditional or period-style toilets have high-level cisterns with an extended flush pipe connecting to the toilet pan, and reproductions are still available today. More common are low-level cisterns, with a short connecting flush pipe; the recommended height for positioning these varies according to area, but is generally between 800 and 900mm (32 and 36in). Because the pan sits in front of the cistern, this type of arrangement takes up more floor area than a high-level cistern, where the pan can be sited directly underneath. Another standard design is the compact or slim low-level cistern, which is made of plastic rather than porcelain and can be concealed behind a duct or dummy wall, or even a false ceiling. Close-coupled toilets have cisterns that are directly attached to the toilet pan, forming a single unit. There are also corner cisterns, specially designed for awkward spaces.

In functional terms, the two basic types of pan are washdown and siphonic. In the washdown pan, water falling from the cistern and flushed around the rim of the bowl clears waste via a trap filled with water. These type of pans are cheaper and less prone to blockages, but often noisier. In the siphonic pan, flushing is aided by suction, which produces a quieter flush. Some American all-in-one toilets that combine cistern with pan are also ventilated so that smells are expelled along with waste.

Toilet pans can be floor-mounted or wall-hung. Floor-mounted designs come with either a foot or a pedestal. Wall-hung pans can be either secured to a masonry wall or supported by a concealed metal stand.

Comfort

Comfort is always a relative concept and never more so than in the case of toilets. Overcome your self-consciousness and try out different designs in the showroom to discover which feels most natural. The height at which the pan is fixed is obviously a key factor – the standardized height of a floor-mounted toilet suits a standardized human, but may not suit someone who is much taller or shorter than average, a child being a case in point. Wall hung pans allow you to site the toilet at a height which suits your frame.

Low-level toilets have long been recommended as more conducive to peristalsis, as they force you to adopt a position

closer to squatting. People from cultures where a squatting position is the norm often find it hard to adapt to the typically high-level Western toilet – and vice versa. Low-level toilets are not so good for urinating men, however, because they increase the likelihood of splashing. In Germany, it is not unusual for private bathrooms to include wall-mounted urinals. This is perhaps not surprising, as German toilet pans typically include a horizontal ledge – a sort of inspection shelf – which effectively ensures that unless your aim is very good splashing is inevitable. You should also take into account the necessary clearance at the front and at the sides for the legs. Some corner toilets incorporate a seat which can be shifted 45 degrees left or right if space is tight on one side.

The shape and contour of the toilet seat can make a big impact on immediate comfort. This is taken to the extreme in certain Japanese designs which include integral heating, as well as jets of water and air to cleanse and dry: half toilet, half bidet. Seat hinges that extend right the way across minimize the chance of the seat working loose. Hydraulic hinges, which lower the seat gently, are also available.

Materials

Porcelain or vitreous china remains the standard material for both the toilet and the bidet. Cisterns may be either porcelain or plastic. Stainless-steel toilets, of the sort often specified in hospitals, prisons, or other institutions, are another option. These are often constructed with integral rims; alternatively, they can be fitted with clear acrylic seats. Most toilet seats are opaque acrylic, although wood remains a popular option as a choice of material.

Bidets

Once almost unknown in British and American households, the bidet is now a more common part of the standard bathroom suite, as it has been in continental Europe for many decades. Even so, if space is tight, this is the one fixture which is likely to be forgone.

Although superior showers and vastly improved standards of personal care mean that the bidet is no longer, strictly speaking, necessary, it remains more hygienic to wash after using the toilet rather than to wipe with paper. Bidets, like toilets, are usually made of vitreous china and designed to match. They may be wall-hung or floor-mounted. The standard and simplest types are designed so that you sit facing the taps (faucets), which means you need to position the bidet where your legs will not be cramped. Other varieties draw water down via a rim or have spray jets. Whichever type you choose, ensure that it is positioned alongside the toilet, for easy access.

ABOVE LEFT Metal fixtures, such as this wall-mounted toilet pan, were originally designed for utilitarian uses in places such as hospitals, prisons and other types of institution. Here, the high-tech aesthetic has been carried over in the crisp black tilework, graphically set off with white grouting. **ABOVE** Toilets used to be fairly standard items of sanitaryware, varying little from range to range. Now, however, they are being designed with as much attention to sculptural form as bathtubs and sinks, as the matching toilet and bidet in pure white ceramic reveal. The bidet is an optional item in the bathroom; if included, it should always be sited near the toilet.

ABOVE Curved forms can seem a natural choice when it comes to making a shower enclosure. This version has an adobe-like quality due to the rendered finish. Waterproof renders are suitable for such applications.

LEFT A custom-made bathtub finished in waterproof render has an over-the-bath shower on a long curving stem. Such arrangements generally include a diverter, so that water can be directed either to the shower or to the bath taps (faucets).

RIGHT Traditional style shower fittings are widely available. Here they complement the original cast-iron bathtub. A pair of shower curtains hangs from a curved metal rail suspended from the ceiling. These should always be tucked inside the tub while showering.

SHOWERS & SHOWER HEADS

Showering is a fast, efficient way of getting clean and ultimately more hygienic than baths because soap and grime are rinsed away under running water. What people want from a shower, however, varies enormously. Some simply want to get wet all over; others don't feel they've had a proper shower unless they've been blasted halfway across the cabinet or cubicle by the force of the spray. Preferences may also vary according to the time of day: a needle-fine shower provides an invigorating wake-up call first thing in the morning, while a more massaging effect might be required to ease strains and stresses in the evening.

As already mentioned, in British households, water has always been supplied indirectly, via a storage cistern, whereas elsewhere in the world it is supplied directly under mains pressure. This means that to achieve sufficient pressure for showering in Britain, there must be at least 3–4m (10–13ft) from the bottom of the storage cistern to the shower head. Even with the assistance of gravity, British showers have traditionally required larger valves and heads to deliver an adequate volume of water and have generally not been adjustable. Today, however, it is possible to enjoy European or American standards of shower efficiency either by converting to a direct mains supply or by installing a pump.

Bear in mind that pumps cannot be installed if you have a combination boiler and no hot-water cylinder: combination boilers can only heat 25 litres (6½ US gallons) per minute, and a power shower can use more than that. Before making a final selection, consult a shower installer or plumber who can advise on your current system and determine which type of pump is most suitable.

Showering is often recommended as a means of saving water, but remember that power showers use much more water than conventional ones. In a household where several power showers a day are taken, water consumption might even exceed that of the equivalent number of baths.

Shower enclosures

There is a wide range of permutations and combinations from which to choose. An early decision is whether you want a shower or wet room, a separate shower cubicle or cabinet within a bathroom, bedroom or cloakroom, or an over-the-bath shower. Unless you are opting for a wet room, which poses its own requirements in terms of waterproofing (see page 94), showers need either to be enclosed in some fashion to prevent adjacent areas becoming soaked or sited remotely from other fixtures and fittings over a 'wet floor'.

The simplest and most space-saving option, an over-the-bath shower, can be enclosed by a rigid bath screen or by a shower curtain. Neither of these options is fully waterproof. Over-the-bath showers can feature either a bath-shower mixer or a fixed-head shower. If you want both, you can fit a diverter so you can switch from one to the other. It is essential to have a non-slip surface at the shower end of the bath – at the very least, a rubber mat.

Shower doors and shower enclosures are generally made from toughened safety glass, which breaks into relatively harmless pebbles like a car windscreen if shattered. Doors may be hinged, pivoting, or sliding; enclosures, designed to fit into a corner, comprise a door and a fixed side panel. 'Frameless' shower doors and enclosures are available for a more minimalist look. Leaking seals and imperfectly waterproofed walls are two common problems with shower installations, so extra care should be taken over finishes and when fixing enclosures to walls. Stand-alone shower cubicles are also available and are often built in one piece for maximum watertightness. Shower trays come in a range of sizes and materials. If you have a power shower, wide wastes to drain large quantities of water are important; double trays are available for large or two-person showers. Ceramic trays are still widely regarded as the best and are very strong and stable. Enamelled steel is very slippery and, where the tray is ridged to improve grip underfoot, grubby limescale deposits can build up. Acrylic trays lack the stability of ceramic. Custom shower trays, made from stone, are expensive, but can be grooved or channelled to provide a non-slip surface and encourage water run-off. Similar designs are available in water-resistant hardwood.

Don't forget to incorporate ledges or recesses for bathroom products and accessories. Soap or shampoo bottles placed on the floor of the shower in default of anywhere else to put them multiply the risk of slipping.

ABOVE This beautifully detailed walk-in double shower room is made of toughened safety glass. The large shower heads set flush in the ceiling have integral lights. **ABOVE RIGHT** A sweeping curve of frosted glass creates a seamless shower enclosure. Water drains via a steel tray. **RIGHT** Panels of frosted glass allow natural light through into the shower area while preserving an element of privacy. Slatted teak provides a handsome non-slip surface over a shower tray, while the generous wall recess offers plenty of space for accessories, shampoos, and soaps.

Shower heads and jets

Shower heads vary widely in size, shape, and design, from large rose heads to small, adjustable jets. Fixed heads are either attached to a visible shower arm or fixed directly to the wall at an appropriate height, with pipework concealed within the wall. Flexible heads have hoses and are attached to a sliding bar so that you can vary the height. Some types of head require a pump to function in Britain. Materials are typically chrome, new brass, and nickel.

Adjustable shower heads allow you to choose the type of spray you want. In most of these heads, the water is aerated, which both reduces water consumption and has a silkier feel on the skin. Strength of spray ranges from needle-fine to full power. Overscaled 'rain' shower heads simulate the effect of standing in a tropical downpour. The most minimal showers consist simply of an upright spout or pipe, angled or curved at the top to release a single stream of water.

Most shower heads are positioned overhead. Side or back jets, where water is directed at the body, are also available – a diverter switches water flow from the main head to the jets. A similar fitting is the vertical 'rain' bar, generally installed in pairs, one either side of the shower. Here, spray emerges from small openings along the length of the bar.

Controls

Temperature control, as much as water flow, is a key element of an efficient shower. The biggest disadvantage of a standard bath-shower mixer, or handheld shower set, is that it can be difficult to maintain the right temperature. A shower that suddenly runs cold can be a shock to the system; one that scalds is downright dangerous. In Britain, variations in shower temperature are more likely to occur if there is a variation in pressure between hot and cold water. Cold water should flow directly from the storage cistern;

hot-water connections should be made as close as possible to the hot-water cylinder to avoid such discrepancies. Control valves generally require concealed pipework, although there are traditional models where the pipework is exposed. The simplest controls regulate temperature only. A lever or disc turns through off to cold, then through warm to hot. Dual-control thermostatic valves enable you to preset the temperature before getting into the shower and to vary the type of water flow. Some models incorporate built-in safety devices so that a child cannot manipulate them and run the risk of scalding. Siting controls outside a shower area can also be an advantage in this respect.

Special features

Showers nowadays boast many of the hydrotherapy features that are also found in spa baths (see page 110). Pulsating or massaging jets can be adjusted to target a specific area of the body or simply provide an overall therapeutic and relaxing effect; jets can also be scented with essential oils; cascades and waterfalls provide a drenching deluge. In the so-called 'Scottish shower', which is available from Jacuzzi, jets deliver alternate bursts of hot and cold. One of the most popular options is converting a shower cubicle into a steam cabinet (see page 111), while built-in seats or benches in larger shower enclosures are another aid to relaxation.

FAR LEFT British shower heads have traditionally taken the form of overscaled watering-can roses, in order to deliver a sufficient volume of water under relatively low pressure. **ABOVE LEFT** Far more sophisticated is this combination of adjustable shower head, body jets, and handheld shower. **ABOVE** The contemporary trend in bathroom fixtures is towards simplicity. This handheld shower was designed by Arne Jacobsen for Vola. **ABOVE RIGHT** 'Rain' showers can be adjusted to create a variety of effects, from fine mist to tropical downpour.

TAPS

There is much more to the design of taps (faucets) than at first meets the eye. Due to the differences between indirect and direct systems of water supply, taps have developed along two distinct paths. In Britain, where water pressure is generally low, taps have traditionally been chunky, with wide bores designed to deliver a sufficient volume of water quickly enough to fill a bath or sink. In Europe and North America, taps have evolved as more elegant and minimal designs: the Vola tap by Arne Jacobsen is a classic example. Unless a British household has been converted to a direct mains water supply, many European and American fittings will not work without a pump.

There are other practical matters to consider before deciding on style or finish. The most crucial is whether the taps will fit the sanitaryware – the two elements are likely to come from different manufacturers and may not be compatible. In terms of positioning, there should be a clear overhang so that water does not dribble down the side of a sink or bath. Wall- or surface-mounted spouts or taps should clear the side of the fixture and send water directly to the waste, otherwise it will glance off the sides and cause splashing. Tap dimensions usually specify both the height of the tap above the basin or surround and the projection or throw from the tap hole to the end of the spout.

ABOVE LEFT Taps (faucets) and other controls should always be easy to manipulate with wet, soapy fingers. **ABOVE RIGHT** The curves of these swan-neck taps form an elegant contrast to the otherwise rectilinear lines of the modern sink. Taps must be positioned carefully so that water flows down the waste rather than splashing over the sides. **RIGHT** A minimal yet rather witty design pairs a simple water spout with bar taps.

Try out taps in a showroom before you make a selection, as ensuring that they are compatible with your chosen fixtures and your existing water supply are not the only considerations. Will it be easy to turn the taps when your fingers are wet and soapy? People with impaired grip may find lever taps easier to use. Also, water conservation is increasingly important. Flow regulators are available which cut flows from taps; taps that aerate water also reduce consumption.

Then there is the question of style. Although every rule can be broken, traditional fittings generally look best with classic bathtub and sink designs, whereas the more minimal form of modern taps works well with contemporary baths and vessel sinks. Gold taps have long been a byword for vulgarity; brass-plated taps require plenty of maintenance. Stainless-steel fittings are currently gaining in popularity over the standard chrome- or nickel-plated cast brass. Nickel has a softer appearance than chrome. It looks more like silver plate and needs an occasional polish.

Sink taps

Cheapest and simplest are pillar taps (faucets), one hot and one cold, which fit a two-hole sink. These can also be used on a three-hole sink, with the central hole either plugged with a stopper or fitted with a pop-up waste.

A three-hole mixer consists of hot and cold valves which mix hot and cold water before the water comes out of the central spout. A pop-up waste may be included in the central tap, or there may be a separate plug and chain.

The most modern option is a monobloc (or centreset) mixer, which is fitted to a single tap hole. Controls on each side of the spout mix the hot and cold water supply; or, there may be a single lever control, along with a pop-up waste. Bidet taps are generally of this latter type, although they have a shorter throw and may incorporate a directional nozzle.

Bath taps

Bathtubs require a greater volume of water than sinks, which means that taps (faucets) must be designed to deliver water fast enough to fill the tub without undue delay. In Britain, this means taps must have bigger feeds than those used elsewhere in the world. While pillar taps can be used for bathtubs, it is generally more comfortable and convenient to opt for a bath filler which mixes hot and cold water before it comes out of the spout.

Bath fillers come in a range of formats: some fit two tap holes; others require three; and there are also designs where the two valves are independent of the spout, which allows you freedom of position.

Bath-shower mixers consist of two valves, a central spout and a handheld shower set (traditionally resting in a cradle above the tap), along with a diverter to switch from bath to shower function. Standard baths generally have an overflow.

Positioning

The basic choice is between fixtures mounted directly to the sanitaryware and those which are positioned elsewhere. In the case of fixtures that are mounted directly to sinks or bathtubs, there must be enough room around the taps (faucets) or valves that they can be turned easily. In addition, the spout must clear the rim by a sufficient margin so there is no risk of water deflection from the sides of the fixture.

Taps and valves mounted on the wall, on a surround, behind the fixture, or freestanding on the floor have a neater appearance. This solution is particularly advisable for freestanding bathtubs, vessel sinks or any other fixtures where taps would interrupt clean lines or sculptural form. Bath taps and shower fixtures on freestanding floor legs are a traditional accompaniment to a rolltop bath; handsome reproduction Victorian or Edwardian models are widely available.

ABOVE LEFT Reconditioned taps (faucets) make the perfect accompaniment to period-style sinks and tubs. **ABOVE RIGHT** This chrome monomixer sink tap designed by Philippe Starck comes in a range of heights. In many modern designs, flow and mix can be controlled by a single lever. **BOTTOM LEFT** Simplicity itself: a sink tap in the form of a pipe. **BOTTOM RIGHT** The KV1 is part of a range of classic modern fittings designed by Arne Jacobsen in the 1960s. Although it is actually a kitchen mixer, it is often used in bathrooms as well.

LIGHTING

Bathroom lighting demands extra care, in terms of both aesthetics and practicality. The most important consideration is safety. Water and electricity are dangerous, potentially lethal, in combination, and the bathroom is where the two come into closest proximity. For this reason, it is always important to consult a qualified electrician when planning a bathroom lighting scheme and to restrict your choice to fixtures specially designed for bathroom use.

The bathroom is a multipurpose area, and lighting should support different activities and moods. You will need bright task light for shaving or putting on make-up and softer ambient lighting for relaxing and recharging your batteries.

Safety restrictions mean that bathroom lighting tends to be fitted, which in turn puts the onus on proper planning and assessment. Unlike other areas in the home, you won't be able to move a light easily if the effect is not what you wanted. Plan the lighting after you have decided where the main fixtures and fittings will go, and take into account lighting conditions in adjacent areas, particularly if the bathroom is en suite, so that they blend well.

LEFT A variety of different light sources have been combined here to mellow effect. Recessed downlights illuminate both the bathroom enclosure and main bedroom. In the bathroom itself, a backlit bath panel and sidelit full-length mirror provide glowing focal points. Light spills through from area to area.

ABOVE RIGHT Where a bathroom immediately adjoins a bedroom, there should not be an abrupt change in either lighting or style from one area to another. Here, shaded wall lights and small pendants in the bedroom, along with the downlit tub and backlit alcove in the bathroom, create a restful mood.

RIGHT Underlighting serves as an evocative way of signalling the change in level between bathroom and sleeping area.

Safety

Regulations vary from country to country, so it is best to consult an electrician to find out whether what you are planning is safe and legal. In the United States, where voltage is low and switches are grounded, normal switches can be used inside the bathroom. In Britain, where voltage is high, it is illegal to have a socket or switch in the bathroom, with the exception of an insulated low-voltage shaver point. All lights must be controlled by a switch outside the room or a pull-cord within it. All bulbs and metal parts of light fixtures must be completely enclosed unless they are at least 2.5m (8ft) away from showers, tubs, or sinks – splashes can cause bulbs to shatter. Avoid pendant lights where the bulb may be splashed and adjustable light fixtures that you might be tempted to move with wet hands. All light fixtures should be steamproof as well as waterproof.

Light sources

Tungsten remains the most common light source in the home. It is typically warming and flattering, with a yellowish cast, and tends to go well with classic, mellow decoration. Tungsten strip lights, sometimes called architectural strips, work well in bathrooms. Halogen, on the other hand, emits a much whiter light which is better at rendering colour

Task lighting

The area around the sink and mirror is where you need the brightest light for shaving, putting on make-up, and general grooming. Very bright task light can be too harsh; very dim light may be flattering, but it simply won't do the job.

The direction of light is just as important as the intensity. Relying solely on top lighting gives a misleading picture and puts years on you, casting heavy shadows on the face. The ideal is an even illumination from all sides, the classic example being the type of arrangement found in a theatrical dressing room, where individual bulbs are mounted round the perimeter of the mirror. You can balance a light over the mirror with wall-mounted lights to either side. There are also bathroom mirrors which incorporate a light source, and some mirrored cabinets have an integral shaving light.

Background light

In the days when the bathroom was a style-free zone, a sole central overhead fixture lit most bathrooms. Few lighting arrangements are more deadening and so lacking in atmosphere: a central overhead source invariably creates a flattened effect. Multiple lights are much more space enhancing, and individual lights need not be very bright to provide the same overall illumination as a single source. Bear in mind that many bathroom surfaces and finishes, from ceramic fixtures to mirror, glass, and tile, are in themselves highly reflective, and a lower level of light minimizes the risk of glare. Fitting a dimmer switch allows you to vary the mood; you may wish to have lights on two different circuits, one for the background lighting and one for task lighting. Fluorescent lights don't dim successfully.

Recessed downlights, strategically positioned to illuminate bathroom fixtures, combine practicality with the potential for mood enhancement. Wall-mounted uplights bounce light off the ceiling and generate a sense of volume. Lights recessed in the floor, in the shower area, or at the base of a bathtub inject an immediate sense of drama.

relationships, hence its widespread use in retail outlets. Halogen sources work well in contemporary interiors or where you are looking for a bright, sparkling effect to enhance the effect of glass, chrome, or crisp, white tile. Low-voltage halogen can be used in the bathroom as long as the bulbs are completely enclosed. Fluorescent light used to be uniformly greenish, but whiter varieties are now available; it can be made more attractive if covered by a warm-coloured gel. This type of light source is often most useful and more attractive when concealed behind a baffle or cover strip to light a vanity top.

The best light source of all is natural light. Top lighting via a skylight is invigorating, particularly if the skylight is positioned over the tub. Windows can be screened with frosted, etched, or coloured glass to admit light while still preserving privacy. If the bathroom lacks a window, borrow natural light from other areas by fitting an internal glazed panel or door in one wall.

ABOVE Bathroom mirrors should be sidelit so the face is evenly illuminated. Top lighting can be misleading and unflattering unless it reflects upwards from a pale surface. **RIGHT** Recessed downlights are reflected in the extensive mirror-clad surfaces, multiplying the effect of light.

Special effects

Light playing on water possesses a magical quality. Many hydrotherapy baths incorporate underwater lighting as one of their features. Other special effects can be achieved with fibre optics. In fibre-optic lighting, light is reflected down thin strands of fibreglass or acrylic to emerge at the tips. The light source itself can be very remote from the light that is actually emitted, which means that such lighting can be safely used in combination with water, to light taps (faucets) or shower heads, for example, or to illuminate the interior of a bath with many starry points of light.

Some bathroom fixtures incorporate backlit translucent plastic panels. These have the effect of dematerializing what otherwise might be bulky installations and create a pleasingly evocative background glow.

Far less high-tech and considerably cheaper are candles and firelight. Tea lights floating in the bath water or church candles massed on the surround or on glass shelving generate an instant sense of relaxation. Scented candles double the sensory benefits.

ABOVE Light and water are magical partners; electricity and water are lethal. Fibre optics is one way in which tubs, sinks, and taps (faucets) can be safely and atmospherically lit.

FAR LEFT Here, an illuminated glass partition creates a soft background glow.

LEFT Bathtubs and vanity units are now available with backlit side panels made of plastic. The effect is to reduce the apparent boxiness of such fixtures.

NEAR LEFT Overhead light sources can cause glare unless they are properly shaded. Here, overhead lighting is diffused through the use of a wide ring of frosted glass, so that the tub is bathed in a gentle light.

HEATING

In the not so distant past, many bathrooms were unheated or heated only minimally, a factor which helped to contribute to their rather punitive atmosphere. In cold or temperate climates, warmth is essential in a bathroom: you want to be able to undress in comfort and step naked and barefoot out of the bath or shower without encountering arctic conditions or a glacial floor. I once had a small central heating radiator installed under my cast-iron tub to warm both the bathroom and the surface to a comfortable temperature, and keep the bath water hot for longer.

There are three main ways of heating a bathroom: with underfloor or undertile concealing heating, with conventional or wall-hung radiators, and with heated towel rails. In every case, you need the services of an experienced, properly qualified plumber or electrician to carry out the installation. This is not the place for skimping.

Underfloor or undertile heating is discreet, space saving, and helps to warm up inherently cold, dense materials such as stone, tile, or concrete used to clad floors or walls. Underfloor systems using hot water require more depth than electrical mat installations. The temperature can be set at a low, background level. In larger bathrooms with sufficient floor area, conventional radiators run off the existing central heating system can be used, although convection systems that slot into the floor or the wall at skirting level are less obtrusive. If floor area is more restricted, wall-hung or vertical radiators are more space saving; these are available in a range of formats, from coiled springs to ladder-like designs. Slim, panel radiators can be recessed into a wall and fitted with rails for drying towels as an added benefit.

A heated towel rail on its own is generally not enough to warm an entire bathroom, unless the room is very small. Most heated towel rails can be linked to existing central heating systems. Oil-filled electric rails are also available. If you want to use the rail to warm towels in the summer when central heating is switched off, there are also types incorporating an electric element, which is generally sited in the bottom rail. Heated towel rails come in a range of finishes to complement taps (faucets) and other accessories.

Ventilation

Excessive humidity in the bathroom makes surfaces and finishes deteriorate more quickly. Persistent damp can cause mould, often heralded by a musty smell. Internal bathrooms, by law, must be fitted with mechanical extraction to refresh the air; the fan must be powerful enough to provide the requisite number of air changes per hour given the size of the bathroom. While large bathrooms, with one or more openable windows, may not, strictly speaking, require extra ventilation, a fan is often a useful supplement, both for clearing steam and condensation, and for expelling odours. Many extractor fans are automatically triggered by a light switch and cut off a few minutes after the light is turned off.

FAR LEFT Heated towel rails usefully combine two functions in one. In a bathroom where wall area is restricted, a vertical towel rail is a sensible use of space. **LEFT** The next best thing to a heated towel rail: pegs positioned directly over a box radiator allow towels to be dried in the rising warm air. **BELOW LEFT** The 'Hot Box' is a recent innovation in bathroom heating; the range includes internally heated wall-hung shelves or boxes for towel storage. **BELOW RIGHT** A spiral column radiator is both space saving and eyecatching.

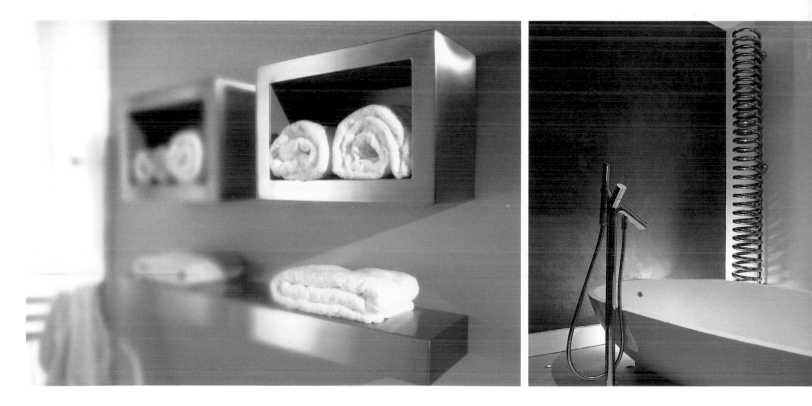

ABOVE Storage needs should always be considered from the outset to avoid a piecemeal look. In this case, a long line of wall-hung units supplies enough space for storing bath linen and cleaning and grooming products. A circular sink is inset in the top, with plenty of room to either side for the display of a few well-chosen objects. The long, low lines and veneered wood finish give an elegant and furnished effect.
ABOVE RIGHT An old wall-hung wooden cabinet provides a means of displaying a collection of bath oils and lotions.

STORAGE

Unlike the kitchen, the other area in the home which has fixed servicing points, the bathroom is generally not required to house a large quantity of possessions or products of wildly differing types. However, what you do keep there is often needed within arm's reach – you don't want to stray far from the sink, for example, to fetch the toothpaste or grab a towel. And while bathrooms may be increasing in size, most are still smaller than living areas and bedrooms, which means that how you organize storage in your bathroom will have more of an immediate impact.

The vogue for Zen-style minimalism, which has had a major influence on the design and fitting of bathrooms, inevitably entails a 'less is more' approach, with storage seamlessly concealed in built-in cupboards or units. Clutter of any description rapidly undermines a sense of relaxation, but some people may find a bathroom almost entirely devoid of any points of visual interest a little too stark and austere. Many of the accessories of personal care are good-looking enough to bear scrutiny – it can even seem a shame to hide them away at times. Attractive containers, jars, and bottles for essential products are where storage meets display.

Assessment

Many people approach the problem of where to put things by buying more things to put things in. This is not necessarily the wrong strategy, but it can easily result in a piecemeal effect. Far better is to consider your storage needs from the outset, as part of the planning process, which means first of all reviewing what you keep in the bathroom. The smaller your bathroom, the more ruthless you should be in terms of the type and quantity of belongings you keep there.

Elsewhere in the home, belongings are often stored on the basis of accessibility and frequency and type of use. In the bathroom, this form of categorization changes slightly. You should not be keeping anything in the bathroom that is not more or less on daily call or is not directly relevant to the activities taking place there. Similarly, you may buy toilet paper or cleaning products in bulk, but that does not mean you have to provide space for your entire supply within the bathroom itself. Otherwise, what you keep in the bathroom generally falls into one of two categories: what you don't mind having on show and what is better concealed. The precise location of that dividing line is, of course, somewhat subjective. Bear in mind that closed or concealed storage may be required for things which deteriorate in damp, humid conditions or certain medicines or remedies which are best stored in the dark or out of reach of children.

Strict minimalists import even their toothbrushes from storage caches outside the bathroom; for the rest of us, there are a certain number of basic necessities which we prefer to keep at hand. All bathrooms (aside, perhaps, from small wet rooms) should include places to hang or store towels, and a means of organizing spare rolls of toilet paper, grooming products (soap, shampoo, bath oils, and so on) and cleaning products. Cloakrooms or guest bathrooms require the minimum; family or shared bathrooms will obviously need more generous storage provision.

Many people like to keep medicines, first-aid supplies, and other home remedies in the bathroom, partly because there is ready access to water and partly because a higher standard of hygiene generally prevails here than in other areas of the home. Some medicines, however, such as certain cosmetics, deteriorate more rapidly if they are subject to hot, steamy conditions and thus may be better stored elsewhere. In any case, if you do include a lockable medicine cabinet, you should periodically go through it and discard any old or half-finished supplies which might be at best ineffective and at worst downright harmful.

Cosmetics and beauty products can accumulate rapidly, particularly if teenagers are sharing the bathroom. Tastes are fickle at this age and brand allegiances swapped in the blink of an eye, which means you may soon face a skyline of different shampoo bottles, each three-quarters full. If your bathroom is starting to resemble the personal care section of a supermarket, it's time to call a halt to experimentation – or to insist that such products be kept in the offender's bedroom where everyone else won't have to look at them.

Like medicine, make-up and cosmetics have a rather limited shelf life: in time, nail varnish goes tacky, mascara dries up, and creams spoil. Weeding out what is past its use-by date at regular intervals will help to keep you ahead of the game. Otherwise, there's no law that says the bathroom must serve as a make-up area. If that function threatens to override every other aspect, it might be worth setting up a dressing-cum-make-up area in a bedroom. This means that time devoted to grooming will not be at the expense of other family members' access to the bathroom.

It is reasonable to keep a few cleaning products in the bathroom. As the place which serves basic bodily functions, the bathroom is where we are most acutely aware of any shortfalls of hygiene. Having bleach, cleansers, cloths, and brushes on hand to remedy the situation makes more sense than having to dash off and retrieve such items from a remote location. If a large, shared bathroom includes laundry facilities, you will need additional storage for soap powders and the like. It makes a routine chore more seamless if the laundry basket or hamper is also located here.

Types of storage

Built-in storage makes good sense in the bathroom. It is both a means of concealing what you do not particularly want on view – which can include features such as plumbing runs and the undersides of sinks, as well as belongings and products – and a means of integrating separate fixtures into

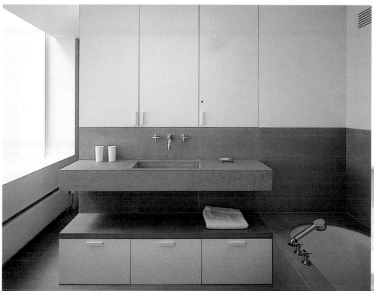

a well-considered architectural framework. Even in a small bathroom, the sacrifice of a certain amount of floor area to built-in storage can neaten the layout to the extent that the overall area appears more spacious than it did before. Opting for back-to-the-wall toilet pans and wall-hung sinks, where the cistern, soil stack, and pipework are hidden behind a dummy wall or duct, allows you to build in storage provision as well, in the form of recesses, cupboards, or shelves.

The most common site for built-in bathroom storage is under the sink. There is a wide range of vanity units on the market in a host of different finishes, materials, and styles, from standard laminate to solid wood. New designs can have the long, low lines of a retro sideboard and may be either poised on visible legs or wall-hung, both of which are space enhancing in effect. If you are very short of space, however, the only option may be a simple wall-hung cabinet, but even here you do not have to sacrifice style.

An alcove or recess can similarly be exploited as a place for built-in storage. Many bathroom products and accessories do not require deep storage; tall, shallow cupboards lined with shelves make practical repositories. Alternatively, you can position storage units in such a way as to define different areas within the bathroom. A pair of tall cupboards can be placed so that they flank a sink and vanity top; a full- or half-height partition screening a toilet from the rest of the bathroom can incorporate storage provision on its facing side.

FAR LEFT This cabinet, screened by a frosted-glass panel, has been neatly integrated into a partition wall separating the toilet from the rest of the bathroom. **LEFT** Suspended units are visually lighter than those which extend to the floor. Here, that lightness is enhanced by the white lacquered finish and semi-transparent perspex panels. **ABOVE LEFT** A seamless approach to storage marries extensive flush cabinets over the sink with a foot-locker-type arrangement beneath. **ABOVE RIGHT** An alcove to one side of a bay window is fitted out with shelves for linen storage.

ABOVE In a Lebanese bathroom, patterned paper covers cupboard doors on a wall devoted entirely to storage. Special wallpapers for bathroom use are widely available; these have a vinyl coating which is water-resistant. RIGHT Floor-to-ceiling cupboards provide generous space for storage. A kick-stop at the bottom of one cupboard door protects the adjacent glass shower screen.

Dressing rooms

Bracketing clothes storage with bathrooms makes good practical sense and can free up space within the bedroom itself. It is essential, however, to ensure that such storage areas are well ventilated, otherwise clothing could become damp or mildewed. In a large, open-plan bedroom/bathroom or generous living bathroom, you can devote an entire wall to built-in wardrobe space, customized with hanging rails, shelves, and cubbyholes. Where space is more restricted, dressing areas can form connecting suites or vestibules to the bathroom, with facing walls fitted out accordingly.

Storage specifics

▶ Soap needs to dry out between use to avoid it becoming mushy and should be kept on a wire rack or in a perforated or ribbed dish so that water drains off.

▶ Toothbrushes should be kept by the sink, suspended in a wall-mounted toothbrush holder or similar design where they can drain after use. Standing toothbrushes upright in a mug or glass will result in an offensive sludge collecting in the bottom. In a shared bathroom, colour-code toothbrushes so that no one uses the wrong toothbrush by mistake.

▶ The bath rack that bridges the sides of a tub is a traditional means of bringing accessories and necessities within reach, and provides a convenient ledge on which to prop a book.

▶ Individual baskets or sponge bags hanging from a peg rail can be useful for organizing the bathing accessories of different family members in a shared bathroom.

▶ Small containers, coordinated by colour, material, or both, can be used to organize make-up and cosmetics.

▶ Bathroom trolleys provide mobile storage for essentials, including spare towels.

▶ Medicines and toxic cleansers should be kept in locked cupboards or cabinets, preferably out of easy reach, if there are children in the home.

▶ One German supplier markets a mini fridge designed for bathroom use. Storing face creams, cosmetics, and medicines in chilled conditions prolongs their shelf life. Otherwise, a cold glass of champagne and a hot bath go very well together.

Freestanding or unfitted storage pieces work best in larger bathrooms, where they can be sited with clear breathing space round them. Old armoires and chests can do duty as linen stores; utilitarian metal school or sports lockers and salvaged dental or medical cabinets have a quirky appeal.

Much of what you need to keep in a bathroom is eminently shelvable. Glass is a favourite material for bathroom shelving – its transparency does not intrude visually and complements the display of attractive bottles and containers. Also, if cosmetics leak or spill, it won't be stained or damaged. Glass shelving over sinks should have upstanding chrome or metal rims or rails to prevent bottles from accidentally sliding off and smashing in the sink.

LEFT Here, a sliding shoe-storage unit doubles up as the bathroom door. Reflected in the bathroom mirror are hanging rails and shelves. The dressing area itself also incorporates a large floor-to-ceiling mirror to the right of the connecting door. **ABOVE LEFT** Baskets are an economical and simple way of organizing belongings and accessories. **ABOVE RIGHT** A red-cross bathroom cabinet adds both a vivid accent of colour and a touch of humour. **BELOW** A charming array of old salvaged boxes are fixed to a corrugated-iron wall in this Australian bathroom.

Decoration and detail bring the bathroom to life. The bathroom may be first and foremost a functional place, but this does not mean that it should be decorated solely from a standpoint of utility. Colour, pattern, and texture still have their own roles to play, both when it comes to generating atmosphere and in the expression of personal style. And if there is nothing particularly wrong with existing bathroom fixtures, or if there is not enough in the budget to replace them, decoration can be an economical and effective way of putting a new face on things without having to spend too much money.

The repertoire of materials used in bathroom decoration has broadened considerably in recent years. Practicality, however, is still an important issue. Bathroom surfaces and finishes need to be as water- and damp-resistant as possible, which means not only choosing the right treatment or material for the function it has to fulfil, but also ensuring that joints or seams where one surface meets another are fully sealed.

DECOR & DETAIL

DECORATING STRATEGY

In terms of choice of finishes, bathrooms may impose particular constraints with regard to practicality, but the basic decorative strategy is not much different than it is for any other area in the home. The main variables are colour, pattern, and texture – and, more often than not, all three combine in a particular material choice.

Decoration can be used in a positive way, to enhance the qualities of the space, or remedially, to overcome perceived drawbacks. Before you come up with a scheme or make your final selection, think about existing conditions.

Size is always a key consideration when it comes to bathroom decor. Small areas can take only a limited amount of strong colour or overt pattern before they start to feel claustrophobic. In lots of cases, where your bathroom is limited in size, sticking to the same colour or the same material throughout will help to increase the room's overall sense of spaciousness. Larger areas give you a freer hand decoratively speaking and permit more obvious changes from material to material. This is where the use of warm or vivid colours can come in, as they generate a sense of enclosure, in turn adding to the intimacy of a larger space.

A related issue is the quality of natural light. Rooms which have north-facing aspects (or south-facing in the southern hemisphere) have a whiter, chillier light than rooms which face south or west. In such circumstances, opt for warmer colours, and avoid the cooler tones of blue and white, which will only accentuate the inherent coldness. How much light a bathroom receives is another important factor. In a room which has few windows, or windows of restricted size, pale tones will make the available light go further. Bathrooms or cloakrooms that are fully internal need especial care in this respect. Bear in mind that some colours look very different at different times of the day, as well as under artificial light, and you may need to paint test patches or assemble swatches in situ to gauge the extent to which tonal values shift throughout the day.

No area in the home these days is entirely immune from the influences of fashion. Indeed, trends come and go almost as quickly in interior design as they do in clothing. Bathrooms, however, being essentially fitted spaces, cannot be made over quite as easily or as frequently as other rooms. Before you commit yourself to a decorative choice that is very much of-the-moment, ask yourself whether you will tire of it sooner rather than later.

When redecoration is all you can afford, think about where money and effort would be best spent. Ideas for quick and easy makeovers include:
- painting or papering
- concealing existing piperuns with cladding or panelling
- replacing or upgrading the flooring – if the bathroom is on the small side, you may be able to invest in a more expensive material than you would normally be able to afford
- replacing or painting the doors of existing units or built-in storage – for example, laminate can be covered up with special paint; alternatively, you could replace cheap doors with solid wood or glass versions
- painting tilework with special tile paint if you don't like the existing colour or pattern
- improving artificial lighting – this can have a big impact. You may be able to install downlights relatively easily by lowering a ceiling
- upgrading details and accessories – new taps (faucets), handles, towel rails, storage containers, bathmats, and towels inject an instant sense of style

RIGHT A contemporary version of the classic rolltop bathtub is positioned in an alcove tiled with white, round mosaic, and in front of double doors which lead to a sunny outdoor terrace. The light fitting is a design by Inflate called UFO.

Colour

One of the most expressive elements in the decorative repertoire, colour evokes personal responses along with cultural associations and meanings. It has a unique power to generate mood and atmosphere.

White is the default colour of bathroom decor. It isn't hard to see why. White has strong connotations of both purity and utility; it not only suggests hygiene, but also demands a high standard of cleanliness to keep its pristine appearance. While white can be chilly and clinical where there is a poor quality of light, in the right context it is supremely luxurious, ethereal, and restful. An all-white decor can be livened up with small doses of strong accent colour; in combination with other colours, it provides a touch of freshness and essential breathing space. White and black are striking graphic partners.

With its natural association with water, blue is another popular bathroom colour. Inherently restful, cool, soothing, and distancing, it's perfect for creating the mindset for calm contemplation; in partnership with white, it has a jaunty maritime quality. A great deal depends on the precise shade. Blues which contain a hint of red or green are warmer than blue-greys, which can create a chilly environment if the quality of natural light is less than ideal.

LEFT Natural light is diffused through panels of sheer white fabric, enhancing the moody blue-grey used on the wall.
ABOVE A panel of Delft tiles adds definition to a bathroom located under the eaves. A distancing shade, blue helps to make small spaces seem less confined.
ABOVE RIGHT Bright yellow used to pick out a recess contrasts strongly to green mosaic walls.

ABOVE Large expanses of exposed concrete and polished plaster can be a little austere and chilly in a bathroom. Here walls painted a warm raspberry pink provide a softening touch that helps to dispel any feeling of heaviness or monumentality.

The warmer part of the spectrum – including red and orange – comprises shades that are both more energizing and more enclosing. Until recently, such strong, vivid colours were infrequently used in bathroom decor, perhaps because they are a little too suggestive of high alert for a room which should ideally be about relaxing and taking one's time. Used to pick out a single surface or plane, and in combination with cooler background tones so that they are not overpowering, red and orange can, however, add a welcome dimension of warmth and vitality to a room's decor.

Like red, green needs both the right context and careful handling. In sunny bathrooms, the paler shades of green can be refreshing and soothing. Where the light is poor, however, such colours can be a little bilious and institutional-looking. Deep, rich greens suggest a certain opulence, but they need to be mediated with plenty of white.

Edgy shades that hover on the cusp between one colour and the next, and which often embrace both warm and cool tones – colours such as pale pink, eau de nil, aquamarine, lavender – can be highly effective in bathrooms, particularly when combined with pure white fixtures. These shades vary dramatically depending on light conditions, an inherent ambiguity that generates mood and atmosphere.

Natural and neutral colours make the perfect backdrop for bathrooms that feature expanses of natural surfaces or finishes. Yellow and terracotta have an earthy quality suited to rustic decor; paler cream or biscuit shades marry well with a cool contemporary style expressed in limestone or wood.

LEFT Colour is used effectively to pick out a built-in bathtub. The rich tone of the framing wall adds a sense of definition, while the interior of the enclosure is painted light yellow with a pale blue ceiling to counter any sense of confinement.

BELOW The appearance of colour varies widely according to finish. The high-gloss effect of the back-painted glass cladding on the walls has a chic, luminous quality. The matt finish as much as the blue-grey colour used elsewhere is more reticent.

ABOVE Op Art patterns laminated on to a wall-hung double vanity unit are reflected in the panels of mirror that are used to clad the wall behind.

RIGHT Even more overt is this Sixties-inspired wallpaper in graphic black and white. Both the geometrical element of the pattern and the use of black and white are echoed in the choice of towels.

FAR RIGHT Used in the wrong way, gold can be a byword for vulgarity, especially when it comes to the bathroom. That is far from the case here, where frosted glass and red mosaic are utilized to provide a sharp-edged contrast to the luminous gold surface of the walls.

Pattern and texture

Patterns that are figurative or based on a motif, rather than designs which are geometric, are closely tied into the fashion cycle and thus liable to date faster than other decorative elements. In a relatively small space, pattern can also be disproportionately attention-seeking, which means it needs to be used with a certain amount of restraint.

At its most minimal, pattern can be introduced in the form of a contrasting border or band of tilework, or as a patchwork of randomly coloured mosaic: in this context, even the grid of plain tiles or single-colour mosaic constitutes a pattern of a sort. Using pattern in this way, either to define or to inject a sense of rhythm that breaks up a surface, can be the best option if space is limited.

Overt or expressive pattern is often more successful on the floor than on other surfaces where it might prove too enclosing or distracting. Traditional Moorish floor tiles, for example, can add an element of richness in an otherwise contemporary space; crisp black and white tiles or mosaic laid in a geometric pattern provide a graphic edge.

In recent years, digitally transferred photographic images have introduced a witty hyper-realism to pattern-making. Ceramic tiles featuring images of sea shells or flowers can be inset in plain backgrounds, while photographic floor tiles simulate the effect of walking on a beach, through a meadow, through leaves, or on water.

We are more acutely aware of texture in the bathroom than in many other areas of the home for the simple reason that, barefoot or undressed, we are more exposed to it. For reasons of practicality and comfort – not to mention safety – you should avoid surfaces that are excessively rough, which might graze your skin. At the same time, floors and any area which is liable to become wet need to provide sufficient grip underfoot that you do not slip.

Subtle variations in texture are a good way of bringing character and interest to an otherwise plain or neutral scheme. A wooden vanity top, for example, provides both visual and textural warmth where other surfaces employed are uniformly smooth and hard.

SURFACES & FINISHES

To a great extent, bathroom decoration is expressed in the choice of materials for surfaces and finishes. Today, the scope is much wider than it has ever been before, embracing glass, steel, wood, stone, and the latest synthetics, as well as more conventional finishes such as cork, marble, laminate, ceramic, and linoleum.

Before you commit to a final choice, you need to think about the following issues:

Maintenance Will the material you wish to use require constant upkeep or special maintenance?

Fitting and installation Most solid non-synthetic materials require specialist fitting or laying, and you should factor the cost of such work into your budget.

Water resistance Will the material provide adequate water resistance where you intend to use it? Any material used in a wet area must be fully waterproof.

Weight Will the material increase loads on the existing floor structure to the point that it needs strengthening?

Warmth Can the material be used in conjunction with underfloor heating? Is it excessively cold?

Cost Many of the most evocative materials are also the most expensive: stone, in particular, can be very pricey. That being said, if your bathroom is not very large, you may well be able to afford a more expensive material here, where you will not require so much of it, than would be the case if you were considering its use elsewhere in the home.

Safety Will the material provide adequate slip-resistance underfoot if you are using it as flooring?

ABOVE LEFT We are far more aware of textural contrast in the bathroom than in many other areas in the home.
LEFT Concrete surfaces bearing the marks of shuttering and formwork have a lively surface texture, here contrasted with clear and frosted glass panels.
RIGHT Concrete, stone, mosaic, and wood combine to create depth of character.

ABOVE Wood is an incredibly varied material. Depending on species, finish, and application, it can be classic, contemporary, or country. Tongue-and-groove panelling painted white makes a crisp and simple wall treatment in a country bathroom.

RIGHT Rough, unfinished planking has a more obvious rural aesthetic, reminiscent of Scandinavian vernacular.

FAR RIGHT Sleek, dark hardwood veneered panels used to clad the side of the bath and vanity unit have a modern appeal.

Preparation

Sound preparation is always important before you begin to install final surfaces or finishes, but it is particularly critical in the bathroom. Many bathrooms feature areas which are clad in rigid materials such as tiles or mosaic. If the underlying floor or wall is not even, level, or straight, tilework will be an irregular eyesore. Where walls are very battered or out of true, you may need to have them replastered before cladding in stone or tile. Floors may need to be lined with hardboard or marine ply to remove surface irregularities. You might consider concealing battered or skewed walls behind tongue-and-groove panelling or a dummy wall. Where walls or portions of walls are to be painted, it is important that the surface is smooth and free of superficial cracks or dents, otherwise water may penetrate beneath the paint and cause it to lift.

Pay particular attention to the joins between fixtures and walls, and the seams between different materials. Always use recommended waterproof sealants and grout to prevent water seeping behind fixtures and into underlying surfaces or structure, where it might cause rot. Where a certain amount of give is unavoidable, you may need to fix a cover strip over the join to ensure full watertightness.

Wood

The patterning of the grain, the rich, warm tones, and the way wood acquires depth of character with age and use are all strong aesthetic recommendations, making it one of the most appealing of all natural materials. Its sheer familiarity as both construction material and final finish evokes a certain sense of domestic comfort. As it is derived from a living source, wood contains a high percentage of water. Before use, it must be dried or 'seasoned' until the moisture content stabilizes with surrounding conditions. Most commercial timber is dried (artificially or naturally) to a moisture content of around 10 per cent. Still, the process of seasoning never entirely stops, which means that timber is susceptible to changes in warmth and humidity. All solid timber will expand and contract across its grain. Excess damp can cause wood to swell and warp and eventually rot and decay.

Wood used in a bathroom must be carefully selected and properly treated. Suitable species include naturally water-resistant cedar and teak. Hardwoods in general are more durable and water-resistant than softwoods, but you must ensure they come from sustainable sources – many tropical hardwoods are endangered in the wild. Manufactured woods, such as marine ply, where the ply layers are bonded with waterproof glue, as well as exterior grades of ply, are more economical. Yacht varnish provides additional protection.

Timber flooring specially designed for bathroom use is also available. In my bathroom in the country, the wooden floor consists of two layers of pale-grey Austrian oak with a layer of ply sandwiched between; the result will not warp or stain if it gets wet. A proprietary oil dressing is applied on top.

Softwood and most types of manufactured wood, such as MDF, are best painted or sealed with yacht varnish. Tongue-and-groove boarding is a relatively inexpensive way to clad the sides of baths and conceal pipework. The tongues and the grooves allow it to expand and contract.

Paint

Paint is a conventional treatment for ceilings and walls not immediately adjacent to wet areas. As bathrooms are prone to condensation, it is advisable to use paints specially formulated for bathroom use, which contain vinyl and may also include a fungicide. These are available in a range of finishes, from matt to sheen, and in a full range of colours.

Existing floorboards can be painted for a quick and easy cover-up. The boards must be stripped of previous finishes, such as varnish, made good by filling in cracks and punching down nailheads, and sanded for an even, smooth finish. An oil-based primer should be applied first, followed by a couple of coats of oil-based paint, such as gloss. Eggshell can also be used, but will not be as durable. For extra water- and wear-resistance, choose yacht paint.

Paint can also be used to revamp other surfaces and finishes if you do not want to go to the expense of complete redecoration. Tiles can be painted with special tile paint, after the initial application of a primer to provide a key. Similar formulations are available for decorating laminate units. Oil-based eggshell or gloss is the standard finish for tongue-and-groove panelling, skirting boards, and other elements made of softwood, and for manufactured woods such as medium-density fibreboard (MDF), often used in construction of dummy walls or built-in storage.

Paper

Properly hung, paper has the advantage of concealing minor imperfections in the surface of the walls, but it is best used away from wet or steamy areas where it is more likely to lift. Paper designed for bathroom use has a vinyl coating to improve water-resistance.

Plaster and concrete

Exposed plaster or concrete surfaces have a raw, organic quality. Standard plaster needs to be coated with a waterproof seal. Alternatively, you can opt for the more water-resistant varieties, including plasters and renders used on the interior of swimming pools. One such product incorporates marble dust. Waxing and polishing creates a smooth, sleek effect. Similarly, concrete will stain readily if it is not properly sealed.

Specialist contractors can cast concrete floors and built-in features such as vanity tops and bathtubs in situ. The final surface may be polished, patterned, grained, or textured, depending on the type of formwork, the components of the basic mix, and the means of finishing. Precast slabs and tiles are also available. As with any heavy, dense material, weight is a prime consideration, and advice may be needed if loads on existing structures will increase appreciably.

Stone

A material with considerable presence, stone is available in many different forms; depending on the type and finish, it can be rustic or patrician, opulent or stark, antique or contemporary. Marble is the stone most traditionally associated with bathroom use, in which application it has become something of a byword for extravagance. The cool, classic beauty of limestone is increasingly favoured in contemporary designs. Slate comes in dark, moody shades and works well in both country and city contexts, while granite has an appealing flecked and mottled appearance and is available in a range of strong colours.

Stone is generally expensive, with prices reaching astronomical heights in the case of solid slabs of imported stone. It is available in a range of thicknesses and formats suitable for different applications, from thin wall tiles to thicker tiles or slabs for floors. Always use a professional to install stone surfaces and finishes, as the material is unwieldy and prone to cracking. Small tiles are generally stuck with adhesive; larger formats require steel fixings. Depending on thickness, weight might be an issue, especially where stone is employed over large areas. You may need to check with a surveyor to determine if the existing structure can bear the additional load.

Vanity tops or splashbacks in stone can be cut to order to provide a seamless integral surface. And remember, salvage yards and monumental masons can be excellent sources of reclaimed or offcut stone.

BELOW Concrete surfaces, tubs, and sinks can be cast in situ by specialist contractors. This tub incorporates steps to either side and is sited under a long, narrow window whose shape echoes the form of the design. RIGHT Marble, slate, and limestone are types of stone commonly used in bathrooms.

LEFT A large panel of frosted glass suspended from a rail can be slid across to separate a bathroom from the bedroom without loss of light.
RIGHT Metal is a material with utilitarian overtones, but this does not mean that extensive use of it in a bathroom need result in a forbidding or clinical, institutional effect. Wise use is the key. The soft sheen of the aluminium panelling here contrasts with a ceramic sink and wooden side table.

Stone is naturally water-resistant – slate exceptionally so – but many types of stone, including limestone and marble, are prone to staining, which means that applying protective dressing is advisable. Consult your supplier for a list of recommended sealants.

Slipperiness will depend on the finish. Highly polished marble or granite is not recommended for flooring applications; honed or sanded finishes are preferable. Slate can be split into layers – or riven – which produces a textured surface.

Stone has great thermal mass, which means it heats slowly, but retains that heat for a long time. In cool climates, stone may be unacceptably chilly without underfloor or undertile heating; in warm climates, the coolness is an asset.

Glass

Recent technological developments for jointing, toughening, and shaping have considerably broadened the use of glass in the home, and bathrooms are no exception to this. Glass sinks and bathtubs are the ultimate in contemporary style; glass partitions and infills maximize natural light while providing an essential screen for wet or humid areas. Extensive use of glass in the bathroom can, however, be a little too hard-edged and chilly; and safety is another

issue. Any frameless glass that you do use should have ground and rounded edges to prevent accidents.

There are many different types of glass, which vary in performance and appearance. Again, a key consideration is safety. Where glass is used as a partition or screen, or as part of a shower enclosure, it should provide the required strength and impact resistance. In the event of breakage, any glass used should disintegrate into harmless pebbles or dice, in the same fashion as a car windscreen. The safest types of glass are toughened and laminated. Toughened glass, also known as tempered glass, is five times stronger than ordinary glass and breaks into relatively harmless pieces. Laminated glass, which is even safer and stronger – and more expensive – consists of a transparent layer of plastic sandwiched between two sheets of glass. The plastic holds crazed fragments in place after impact or breakage. The strongest and safest of all is glass which is composed of both toughened and laminated layers. Careful specification of material and supporting framework is essential.

Safety and strength are not the only performance variables. Low-emissivity, or low-E, glass is an insulating material which prevents excess heat loss where glazing is extensive. Another type of glass turns from transparent to opaque at the flick of a switch, as a result of an electric current passing between the layers. Photosensitive glass, which reacts to light intensity, is also available.

Frosted, etched, and coloured glass obscure views while admitting light. These types of glass maintain privacy and are also recommended for any application where the ambiguity of transparent glass might result in an accident.

Glass blocks or bricks, which come in a range of colours and finishes, from clear to frosted to rippled, can be used to make structural walls, non structural partitions or simply as infills. A somewhat clichéd element of contemporary decor, this material has more presence when used whole-heartedly.

Glass undoubtedly entails more maintenance than other materials. While certain makes of glass sinks have a water-resistant coating which shrugs off splashes and toothpaste, glass partitions and surrounds will need more or less constant upkeep to prevent spotting and streaking. (For mirrors, see page 202.)

Metal
Surfaces and finishes made of metal have a no-nonsense, hard-edged aesthetic: too much and the bathroom can become cold and clinical. Steel is water-resistant but prone to scratching, and it needs regular cleaning and polishing with a proprietary product. Rather more low-tech are sheets of corrugated anodized aluminium, often employed for cladding or roofing rural buildings. This utilitarian material can be used to make simple partitions and shower enclosures.

Tile and mosaic
Tiling remains the most popular way of wetproofing areas around sinks and bathtubs. Ceramic tiles are durable, easy to handle, easy to maintain, readily available, and come in a wide range of sizes, finishes, colours, and designs. Floor tiles have a non-slip surface and are thicker than wall tiles. A degree of skill is required for successful results, and professional installation is recommended. Tiles are generally affordable, but hand-glazed tiles, which have more character than mass-produced versions, can be very expensive.

The most common sizes for wall tiles are 100mm (4in) and 150mm (6in) square; smaller tiles often come in sheet form for easy application. Other varieties include hexagonal tiles and rectangular 'metro' versions with bevelled edges, which have a retro look. Beadings and other forms of edge trim are widely available.

Tiles are a traditional means of decoration and come in many textures and designs, from exotic, ethnic, or period-style motifs to digitally produced photographic imagery. But even a single-colour or plain white-tiled surface has inherent vitality because of the gridded pattern. Grouting tiles with white or black or a colour can change the effect.

Mosaic is essentially tiling on the smallest scale. Most mosaic is made of ceramic, although it may also be made of marble, stone, or glass. Polished marble or glass mosaic

is not suitable for flooring applications, however, because it can be too slippery and therefore not safe.

Mosaic is widely available in sheet form backed with netting or paper, which means that surfaces can be covered relatively quickly and easily. Sheets of mosaic may be single-coloured or feature a random combination of shades or tones; square mosaic is most common, but round mosaic is also available in this type of format. More elaborate mosaic effects featuring geometric patterning or full-scale pictorial motifs can be commissioned from a mosaic artist.

Mosaic is less slippery than ceramic tile – the tight grid of grouting provides better grip underfoot. It is a particularly good way of unifying different surfaces and finishes: custom features, such as specially built bathtubs, can be lined in mosaic to match walls and floors, for an integrated effect.

Composites

Synthetic or composite materials can be used for a number of different bathroom applications. Laminate, for example, is a standard material for vanity tops or built-in surfaces. Some types are composed of layers of paper or pulp bonded with resins under high pressure and heat; others have solid cores. Laminates that are patterned to simulate other, more worthy materials such as natural stone and wood are usually far from convincing. Bright colours and speckled or flecked finishes are more successful.

Corian is a trademarked product made from a blend of acrylic and natural minerals. It is available in a range of materials and thicknesses. It is solid and through-coloured, so patterns and colours do not wear away or peel off, and surface damage can simply be sanded away. It can be cut, drilled, and worked into counters and surrounds.

Another trademarked product is Durat. Like Corian, it is a solid surface board, through-coloured, durable and anti-bacterial; superficial damage can be sanded away. Durat's speckled finish and the large range of colour options available complement the smooth, silky texture; it can be used to construct lengths of seamless, jointless surface with integral sink areas and splashbacks.

Linoleum, vinyl, rubber, and cork

Available in sheet or tile form, linoleum, vinyl, rubber, and cork are standard solutions for bathroom flooring. Tiles are easy for an amateur to lay; sheet produces a more seamless effect, but can be more unwieldy to manage.

Linoleum is a wholly natural product, and both anti-bacterial and hypo-allergenic. Typically smooth, with a matt, grainy appearance, it is available in a range of patterns and colours. It is warm, quiet, and reasonably non-slip.

Vinyl, unlike linoleum, is entirely synthetic, with the better and more expensive grades including a higher proportion of PVC. Designs are often simulations of natural materials such as stone, terracotta, and wood; geometric patterns are more effective. Vinyl is waterproof, but can be damaged by bleach and strong cleansers, as well as cigarette burns.

Most rubber available for interior use is synthetic. Its great advantage is durability and it is also totally waterproof. Modern rubber flooring comes in a huge range of colours; studded or textured finishes reduce the risk of slipping.

Cork is resilient, warm, and quiet. In addition to natural browns, it is available stained or coloured. It is important to opt for presealed cork in thicker grades for floors. New cork tiles faced in vinyl feature a range of photographic images – stones, leaves, flowers, etc – for a tongue-in-cheek effect.

ABOVE FAR LEFT Lozenge-shaped or 'metro' tiles have a retro aesthetic. Here, the tiling extends from floor to ceiling and incorporates matching ceramic mouldings and trim. **ABOVE LEFT** Randomly patterned mosaic adds liveliness and vitality, and is less slippery underfoot than other types of tiling because of its tight grid. **ABOVE** One advantage of rubber flooring is that it comes in almost every conceivable colour.

DETAILS

Details matter. In a functional room, working details – handles, toilet-roll holders, towel rails – must operate efficiently and effectively so that practicality is maintained right down to the most basic level. The accessories of personal care, such as fluffy absorbent towels, scents, and soap, extend the pleasures of bathing into the realms of pure comfort. Decorative touches – or detail as accent – achieve greater prominence in a small space, particularly one that is all-white or neutral in tone. In tandem with new decoration, changing details is both a highly effective way of upgrading the way a bathroom looks and an economical means of responding to contemporary trends.

Window treatments

Bathroom windows require a minimum of dressing or screening – enough to moderate strong light where this is an issue and sufficient to provide the necessary privacy where the bathroom is overlooked. Otherwise, window treatments should be as clean-lined and unfussy as possible. Curtains or elaborate blinds will only trap moisture, which will cause fabric to deteriorate rapidly, and they will also inhibit access to the window unnecessarily. Simple fabric roller or Roman blinds have a neat tailored appearance. If you do want curtains, the less structured headings, such as gathered tucks suspended from rings, are more appropriate than more formal pinched or pleated versions.

There are many other ways of screening a window which do not rely on fabric. Venetian blinds in wood or metal, pivoting vertical louvres, blinds made of split cane – all provide variable light control. Screens made of translucent perspex and slatted wood shutters are other alternatives. Replacing clear window glass with obscured, frosted, etched, or coloured glass, or even mirror, is a popular option in the bathroom; you do not need to replace all the panes to ensure privacy, merely those at the lower level.

Doors

The door is an architectural element which, in terms of style, has an aesthetic impact on the space as a whole and, in terms of operation, affects the workability of layout. If access is awkward, floor area is tight, and layout is necessarily cramped, simply rehanging an existing door so that it opens outwards rather than inwards is a good idea. Similarly, substituting a conventional door for one which slides or folds back can also win you a little extra room. Aesthetics are just as important as practicality. In the bathroom we are perhaps more aware of features such as doors purely because they are much more evident. Poor-quality hollow-core doors are something of a letdown. These can be easily replaced by more substantial solid versions, either panelled or with flush surfaces. Glazed doors or panels serve to borrow light from adjacent areas. Where wall space is limited, the back of the door can be a convenient place for pegs or towel rails – even a toilet-roll holder in a small cloakroom. Whether or not the door should be lockable is a matter of choice. Many people prefer the security this offers, but, in households where there are small children, bathroom locks are a bad idea.

LEFT Panels of acrylic make a discreet and practical window treatment, softening the light and screening views. Other solutions which deliver similar practical and aesthetic advantages include replacing clear panes of glass with frosted or coloured glass. **ABOVE LEFT** A translucent glass panel provides a glimpse of an en suite shower. **ABOVE RIGHT** Bathrooms lend themselves to maritime or nautical themes – although it is important not to overdo it. This internal porthole is all the more appropriate because it frames a sea view beyond.

Mirrors

Whether you are simply checking that your lipstick isn't smudged or require more forensic detail for plucking eyebrows, applying make-up, or shaving, a bathroom mirror is indispensable. Some mirrors are definitely kinder than others; high-specification concave or magnifying mirrors complete with integral lighting can be a little too pitiless for some. The type of mirror you choose – and how much of the bathroom is mirrored – will depend on the amount of exposure with which you feel comfortable.

One of the most common arrangements is the mirrored bathroom cabinet. Like the heated towel rail, this combines two functions in one and makes good use of space if there is limited wall area. Specific features for bathroom use include folding side panels that enable you to view your

profile(s), inset enlarging mirrors for close scrutiny, and heated or demisting elements to prevent condensation. Enlarging mirrors on extendable or concertina arms can usefully supplement an ordinary mirror.

Panels of sheet mirror can be fixed to the wall to dissolve spatial boundaries and enhance natural light. Mirrored tiles create a sparkling effect that fractures and softens views. Remember that large expanses of mirror are heavy and therefore need secure wall anchorage.

Mirrors that are not designed specifically for the bathroom can add decorative flair. Junk shops and salvage yards can be good sources of antique or retro mirrors; ornate Venetian mirrors are particularly popular, and reproductions are easy to find. Framed mirrors should be watertight or condensation will cause rusting.

LEFT Bathroom mirrors vary widely from salvaged or antique versions to the latest high-specification design. These period-style mirrors make a suitable accompaniment to the salvaged sink and taps (faucets).

ABOVE A modern mirror with an inset panel is side-lit, striking the right balance between clarity and flattery. **RIGHT** A custom design incorporates a mirrored circle within a sheet of window glass.

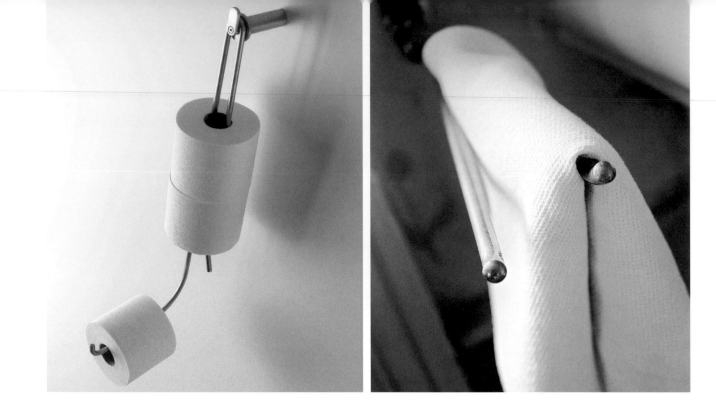

ABOVE LEFT Even such apparently insignificant bathroom accessories as toilet-roll holders now attract design interest. **ABOVE RIGHT** Textured or waffle-weave fabrics tend to be more absorbent than those with smooth or velvet pile. **BELOW** Cotton shower curtains do not stick to the skin in the way the more common plastic varieties do. **RIGHT** Bath linen provides an opportunity for colour coordination.

Shower curtains

Some means of preventing water from splashing on to adjacent surfaces is essential if you do not have a solid shower screen or enclosure. Most shower curtains are made of plastic, and many provide an opening for whimsical patterning. From a practical standpoint, however, cotton shower curtains are better because they do not stick to the skin and drip-dry readily after use.

Towels and bath linen

What goes next to the skin has immeasurable impact. Wet skin loses heat rapidly. Towels should be big enough to wrap up in and absorbent enough to dry you off quickly. Very large bath towels (or 'sheets') obviate the need for towelling robes and are immensely comforting and luxurious. Check sizes before you buy: the dimensions of what are nominally described as 'bath' and 'hand' towels vary considerably.

Quality pays off. Cheap towels, which may seem soft, thick, and fluffy in the store, are often treated with chemicals to improve the way they feel; after a few washes, poor quality will be all too evident. Rather than go by touch alone, examine the towel's weave, which should be densely packed whether it is velvet pile – which tends not to be very absorbent – or the springy loops of terry cloth. Choose waffle weave for maximum absorbency.

Towels are also available in a range of fibres; some include artificial fibres such as polyester to reduce shrinkage. In general, however, natural fibres feel better against the skin, and all-cotton remains a popular choice. Linen in the mix produces a coarser, more exfoliating texture, while cotton blended with silk is exceptionally soft.

The colour selection is vast; simple checked or striped patterns can also introduce a welcome accent. That said, there is nothing more generous or hospitable than a stack of large, pure white towels simply waiting to be used.

Bathmats provide warmth and absorbency underfoot. You can choose between mats coordinated with towels or fabric mats with a deeper, denser pile. Some fabric mats have a non-slip backing. Alternatively, opt for cork or duckboard.

Towel rails and other fittings

Heated towel rails make good practical sense, especially if you are short of space (see page 82). Unheated versions are available in the form of rings or rails. A ring is really only suitable for a guest toilet or cloakroom, which is less frequently used. Check that fixings are robust and secure.

Other fittings range from the more or less indispensable, such as toilet roll holders, to the optional, such as bath racks. In between come handles and catches, wall hooks and glass holders, and a host of other details. In a small room, it is probably best to restrict the number of such fixtures and for them to be as minimal and unobtrusive as possible. Cheaper fittings tend to be made of acrylic or ceramic; upgrading to chrome or brushed-steel versions imparts an immediate sense of quality. Designs encompass the full gamut from the traditional to the more sculptural and cutting-edge.

Display

The accessories of personal care – scents, soaps, and bath products, along with sponges, loofahs, and body brushes – vary in the degree to which they contribute to the overall aesthetics of the bathroom. Beautifully wrapped, handmade soap looks just as good as it feels to use; somehow a bottle of proprietary bath foam lacks the same visual delight. You can also choose to decant products, lotions, and potions into an array of interesting or coordinating storage containers, or jars for a more considered look.

Aesthetic pleasure is not exclusively visual. Scent provides an extra dimension to relaxation. Fragrance has a seasonal aspect as well, with the fresh citrus scents of lemon and lime more welcome and evocative in spring and summer, and heavier, spicier aromas such as cinnamon and sandalwood more comforting in autumn (fall) and winter. Essential oils, which are used in aromatherapy, are ascribed different restorative powers and benefits. Lavender, for example, is said to be calming and soothing; neroli is uplifting; jasmine and ylang ylang are seductive.

If you cannot afford to change much in your bathroom, accessories which serve as visual one-liners provide a wry acknowledgement of other limitations. Items such as a red-cross or pill-shaped bathroom cabinet or Alessi's flowerpot toilet-brush holder inject a little wit and humour without reducing the whimsy to the realm of the ridiculous.

Plants help to lower levels of humidity and bestow a living dimension which is far preferable to ancient, dusty arrangements of potpourri. Choose species such as ferns and orchids that thrive in warm, steamy locations.

Framed prints, photographs, paintings, and other types of artwork make attractive displays, particularly in the more furnished bathroom. As with framed mirrors, these must be watertight to prevent condensation penetrating beneath the glass and spoiling the imagery.

ABOVE Scent has a huge impact on mood and can be an important aid to relaxation. In aromatherapy different scents are ascribed specific benefits and restorative powers. Beautifully wrapped soap provides pleasure on the visual level as well. **RIGHT** A functional bathroom need not be devoid of style. Expressing your personality in terms of decor and detail turns an essential amenity into a welcoming haven.

The following section provides in-depth practical information to enable you to turn inspiration into reality. First, as the bathroom is where many home accidents occur, safety considerations are covered in detail, as are the needs of differently abled bathroom users. Sourcing, buying, and installing a new bathroom can be a complex process – our budget planner, buyer's questionnaire, and advice on commissioning the work will see you through the essential stages. Also, water conservation is increasingly becoming an important environmental issue, so tips are given for ways to reduce water use. Finally, the comprehensive list of suppliers provided at the end of the section will help to steer you in the right direction, whether you're planning a new bathroom or simply upgrading an existing one.

RESOURCES

BUDGET PLANNER

Successful budgeting depends on two factors: prioritizing your needs and preferences, and attention to detail. Unless you are one of the fortunate few for whom money is no object, it's important to spend time thinking about which items on your wish list are essential and which are not. When people overspend, guesstimates and wishful thinking are often to blame. Itemizing every cost, down to the last door handle, will help you to keep track of things and avoid unpleasant surprises.

At the planning stage, draw up a shopping list of preferences, cost them out and then think about where substitutions can be made. Don't be tempted to compromise on basic quality of fixtures and fittings: it's one thing to rule out a custom-made stone bath or a sink with a designer label, quite another to opt for substandard fixtures that will not stay the course. Similarly, it's better to do without a bidet, for example, if that means you can afford a better quality bath, toilet, and sink.

The choice of materials for surfaces and finishes offers the greatest room for financial juggling. Any material, such as glass, which has to be individually specified and supplied to order will naturally be more expensive than materials you can buy off-the-peg at retail outlets. If you find a material is too expensive, think about what you are trying to achieve in terms of texture, colour, and aesthetic when making a substitution. Ceramic tile or mosaic can stand in for stone; renovated floorboards for new hardwood.

Watch out for hidden costs. If a power shower requires a pump, that will have to be factored into your budget, too. If the floor requires strengthening to support a heavy tub, that is also part of the overall financial picture.

Finally, shop around. You may well be able to source basic fixtures and fittings more cheaply. When you are commissioning the work, ask for estimates from a number of properly qualified professionals or tradespeople so you can make price comparisons. Don't be tempted to tackle more of the work yourself than you are able to.

Budget breakdown

▸ Design fees for in-store consultation or architectural service
▸ Financial costs, if you are financing work with a bank loan or hire-purchase agreement
▸ Structural work, including strengthening floors or moving openings
▸ Electrical services
▸ Alterations to water supply and drainage
▸ Installation (plumbing and carpentry)
▸ Charges for delivery and removal
▸ Sanitaryware:
   Bathtub
   Toilet
   Bidet
   Sink(s)
▸ Fixtures and fittings:
   Pump
   Shower head
   Shower tray, cubicle, and screen
   Shower controls
   Bath taps (faucets), diverters, handheld shower fixtures
   Sink taps (faucets)
   Vanity units
   Any special features
▸ Vanity tops, bath surrounds and panels
▸ Splashbacks
▸ Handles, rails, and other accessories
▸ Mirrors
▸ Cabinets and other storage items
▸ Lighting
▸ Heating, including heated towel rails
▸ Laundry machines
▸ Flooring
▸ Decoration – materials and labour

BUYING A BATHROOM

Part of the process of planning and design is acquainting yourself with what is available. Visit a number of different showrooms; collect catalogues and brochures; consult specialist publications to bring yourself up to speed with the current range of designs and technical specifications. If you're after a retro or period look, architectural salvage yards and stores specializing in reclaimed period features can be a good source. Old chipped or discoloured enamel baths can be refinished provided the damage is not too extensive; sometimes this work can be carried out in situ, which is a good idea if your home comes with such period features already installed – moving a cast-iron bath is very heavy work.

Strict coordination is often anathema elsewhere in the home, but in the bathroom it's usually preferable. Although a bold material shift can sometimes be successful, visible fixtures should generally correspond in terms of design and colour. Bathroom fixtures are marketed in ranges or suites which make it simple to come up with a well-considered look once you've made your selection. While making up your mind, don't neglect the issue of fit or comfort. It's well worth overcoming initial embarrassment and actually lying in a showroom tub (or sitting on a showroom loo) to gauge whether or not such fixtures can comfortably accommodate your physical frame.

Many bathroom retailers offer a range of other services, from in-store design to financial plans and fitting. To take advantage of a design service, you will need to take along measurements and details of the position of existing fixtures. The information is entered into a computer program, along with your stated preferences in terms of design, colour, and style of new fixtures. The program then comes up with a detailed three-dimensional representation of the end result.

BUYER'S QUESTIONNAIRE

There is a variety of options when it comes to buying a bathroom. You can go it alone, sourcing individual items yourself and hiring professionals, such as plumbers, electricians, and builders, on a direct basis. If the work is large in scope and you are after a bespoke result, you might consider consulting an architect, who can come up with a scheme to your brief, deal with any necessary permissions and legalities, specify materials, and oversee the project to completion. Alternatively, many specialist bathroom companies offer an in-house design service as well as installation packages. Before you go shopping, draw up a scale plan of the area in question (see pages 34–8), marking on the position of existing fixtures and servicing, and set yourself a budget.

Questions to ask

Is there an in-store design service? Many large retailers offer free design advice. You will need to provide measurements of the area in question, with existing servicing indicated on a diagram or scale plan. Specialist bathroom companies and other design professionals, such as architects, will generally charge for design advice. Most will follow up an initial consultation with a site visit.

Are financing arrangements available? Finance plans which enable you to spread the cost of a new bathroom over a fixed period are provided by some retailers. Compare the cost of borrowing in this way with other types of financing, such as bank loans.

What does the price include? Make sure you are clear what it is you are paying for. All-in-one packages covering the supply as well as the installation of fixtures often do not include additional items such as flooring or tiling, but may have provision for supplying materials and carrying out the work for an additional cost.

Is an installation service available? Larger companies often provide an installation service, which includes removal of old fixtures as well as delivery and installation of new ones. Some specialist companies do not provide such services, but may be able to provide recommendations.

Will my choice of taps fit the sanitaryware? Fixtures and fittings such as taps (faucets), which are produced by different manufacturers, are not always compatible. This may be a particular issue if you are buying a reclaimed or period tub or sink.

Will the shower work without a pump? Before you buy a power shower or some other high-performance feature, find out whether you will also need a pump for it to operate properly. Some pumps are incompatible with certain types of heating system.

Are there special maintenance requirements? If you are buying a tub or sink made out of an unusual material, ask about recommended cleaning products.

Does my choice of fixtures have structural implications? If you have chosen a heavy tub, such as one made of cast iron or stone, you will need to find out whether the bathroom floor structure is strong enough to support it. Similarly, wall-hung fixtures need to be anchored to a solid wall or to brackets concealed behind a dummy panel.

How long will the work take? Installing new bathrooms is disruptive and it is important to know exactly how long you will be without water. If there is only one bathroom in your home, you will need to make alternative arrangements while work is being carried out.

What happens if things go wrong? Companies should provide written guarantees for both fixtures and installation. There should be redress to a complaints procedure if you are not satisfied with the work.

COMMISSIONING THE WORK

In the ordinary course of events, most of us call on plumbers at times of emergency: when a pipe bursts, a drain blocks, or a sink overflows. It is not surprising that, of all the building trades, plumbers are the ones with whom we seem to have particularly fraught relationships. Finding a reputable, affordable plumber in the phone directory while water is pouring through a ceiling is often a domestic challenge too far; tidy livings have been made by less scrupulous plumbing companies who exploit such panic-ridden moments. The extortionate call-out charge, the fee that multiplies with each ticking minute, add insult to injury when the remedy is often a simple case of locating the stopcock and rodding out a blockage. It is small wonder that many people approach alterations that need a plumber's expertise with a degree of trepidation.

The advantage in planning a new bathroom or bathroom alterations is that you can conduct your search for a good professional free from the mounting sense of desperation and blinkered judgement that emergencies often inspire. As is the case with most trades, word of mouth is often the best way of tracking down a trustworthy individual or firm. Ask around. Friends who have had similar work done may be able to point you in the right direction (or steer you away from a disaster). Contrary to popular belief, good, affordable plumbers are not an endangered species, even if they can be a little elusive. The best are often booked up well in advance: don't expect to buy a new bathroom suite one day and have it fitted the next unless you have arranged matters beforehand. Reputable plumbers, like other tradespeople, are generally members of an accredited professional association or federation. This is not a guarantee of good work, but it does give you access to a complaints procedure if things go wrong.

When commissioning work, be specific about what you require, down to the last detail. Most tradespeople have their own preferred suppliers and will generally opt for what is easiest to obtain or what is standard unless directed otherwise. Ask for written estimates which set out in detail fees, the projected schedule, and materials before you agree to give them the work.

Water supply and drainage are strictly regulated. You may need to contact the local buildings inspector or utility board if your plans require alterations to mains drainage or entail new service connections. Your water supplier will have detailed information about the regulations that apply to new connections. The local buildings inspector, on the other hand, controls drainage. New drains must be surveyed and signed off before they are covered up, and inspectors have every right to insist, for example, that new-laid concrete is dug up if you fail to comply.

The sequence of events

Before work begins, make sure you establish how long and how often you can expect disruption to servicing. Living without running water or a flushing toilet for any protracted period places an inordinate strain on most households: know in advance when such disruption is likely to take place so you can make alternative arrangements.

There are a few, rare individuals who are capable on all fronts, able to tackle plumbing, electrical work, and the odd bit of carpentry with equal aplomb. More usually, you will need to secure the services of different tradespeople. This means that you need to know the correct sequence in which the work must be carried out.

Tradespeople who work in close proximity to each other often nurse grievances: plumbers and electricians are among those who have traditionally held such antipathies. Your chosen plumber may well be able to recommend an electrician with whom he or she has worked before; this can be a good way of sidestepping potential disputes and concomitant delays. Cover new bathroom fittings with boards and bubblewrap until all of the work is finished, otherwise they may get chipped or scratched.

All jobs are different, but a typical sequence of work is as follows:
▶ Clearing and demolition
▶ Making new service connections and laying new drains
▶ Structural work
▶ 'First fix' servicing: laying pipework and electric cabling
▶ Basic carpentry
▶ Plastering
▶ 'Second fix' servicing: installing tubs and other fixtures, putting in switches and sockets
▶ Final carpentry
▶ Tiling
▶ Decorative finishes
▶ Flooring

SAFETY CONSIDERATIONS

Alfred Hitchcock famously transformed the shower into a place of ultimate menace. While we might not be vulnerable to the extreme of murderous psychos in our own homes, the bathroom still presents many everyday hazards which need to be addressed in the design process.

Water, particularly soapy water, coming into contact with impervious waterproof surfaces spells increased risk of slipping and falling. That risk multiplies for those who are naturally less steady on their feet, such as young children or the elderly or infirm. A slip in the shower is often enough to put your back out of whack or to give you a nasty bump on the head, at the very least. Bathtubs are available with integral non-slip surfaces, and most shower tray designs are also non-slip. Alternatively, you can provide extra grip with rubber or slatted wood bathmats.

The choice of materials has a role to play in increasing safety. Mosaic, because of its tight grid, provides a better key and grip than large, smooth stone tiles; sealed wood is less slippery than vinyl. Rounded corners and recessed taps (faucets) and other fixtures reduce the risk of injury on a sharp edge.

Thermostatic shower controls that enable temperatures to be preset reduce the likelihood of accidental scalding. Thermostatic controls can also be a good idea for bath taps (faucets), particularly if one of the users has diminished sensation. If young children are using the bathroom, it is best to position such controls where they cannot be tampered with.

The most serious risk in a bathroom, however, is that posed by the proximity of water to electricity. Very strict regulations govern bathroom wiring and the provision of electrical fittings such as laundry machines and lighting. A qualified electrician should always carry out alterations to existing wiring.

In the United States, where voltage is low, electrical sockets are permissible in a bathroom provided they are at least 1.5m (5ft) away from the bathtub and are positioned high up a wall. In Britain, where the voltage is higher, only low-voltage shaver sockets are permissible in a bathroom. In addition, lights must have pull-cords inside the bathroom or switches outside, laundry appliances and metal bathtubs should be earthed, and all electrical appliances should be wired into a fused external power supply.

Special needs

Designing a bathroom for those with special needs means taking a wide variety of factors into account. There is no single solution which is applicable in all cases. Disability or impairment takes many different forms and what would meet the needs of one individual may not address those of another. At the outset, it is essential to make a thorough assessment of requirements, perhaps in consultation with medical professionals or other specialists, who will be able to provide detailed advice.

Flexibility, access, and ease of function are key issues. Where a disability or illness is progressive, it is also important to arrange matters so that the bathroom can be readily adapted in the future without too much additional expense or disruption. This might entail arranging the layout in-line or strengthening ceiling joists to facilitate the later installation of hoists or other pieces of specialist equipment.

Another key factor is expense. Many types of specialist equipment entail both considerable financial outlay and professional installation; you need to make sure the investment will be worth the likely safety benefits over a lifetime of use.

▶ **Siting** Ground-level bathrooms are essential for wheelchair users. If your home is arranged over several levels, providing a toilet on each floor is also a good idea if someone in the household is elderly or finds it difficult to negotiate stairs.

▶ **Access** Wheelchair users require plenty of room to manoeuvre, which means widened doorways (a minimum of 80cm/31in) and generous space around main bathroom fixtures. Wall-hung fixtures are better than pedestal or floor-mounted ones. Whether a door opens inwards or outwards can also make a difference to access and ease of use.

▶ **Bathing and showering** Simple adaptations include fitting a fold-down seat and grab rail to a shower for those who find it difficult to stand for long periods, or fitting a seat and hand grips to a bathtub to make it easier to get in and out.

▶ **Taps and controls** Lever taps (faucets) are much easier to manipulate for those with impaired grip, such as arthritis sufferers. Existing taps can be modified by fitting lever covers over the top. People with reduced sensation are at risk of scalding. Thermostatic controls allow temperatures to be preset at a safe level.

▶ **Surfaces and finishes** Non-slip flooring is essential. Ridged shower trays, as well as rubber bathmats, provide extra grip underfoot. Avoid sharp corners or edges that could provide an additional hazard. Avoid extensive use of mirrored surfaces in a bathroom designed to be used by those with visual impairment – reflections can be confusing and lead to accidents.

▶ **Specialist equipment** There is a wide range of specialist bathroom equipment available, from bath hoists that enable people to be lifted into and out of the bath, to sinks that can be adjusted to different heights.

WATER CONSERVATION

Water is one of our most precious resources. Growing demand worldwide and changing climate patterns mean that supplies are increasingly under threat. We can no longer afford to treat water as if it were limitless nor to ignore the issue of conservation. This is true not only in hot, dry regions, but also in countries where water has until now been plentiful. London, for example, was drier than Rome and Istanbul in the summer of 1996; meanwhile, consumers within the Greater London area are projected to increase by a million over the next 20 years. Bathing and related activities are not the sole means by which water is consumed: in arid areas of the United States, 80 per cent of household water goes on garden irrigation and outdoor chores such as car cleaning.

New legislation, in both Europe and the United States, has tackled one large area of water consumption in the home, which is toilet flushing, estimated to account for 50 per cent of water use in many areas. New toilets must now use no more than 6 litres (1⅗ US gallons) per flush and the limit may well fall further to 4.5 litres (1¼ US gallons). Other countries are either following suit or already have these measures in place. In addition, there are commonsense measures everyone can adopt to use water wisely.

▶ Fix all dripping taps (faucets), worn washers, and leaking cistern valves. Leaks and drips are pure water wastage and add up to a significant proportion of consumption – up to 90 litres (24 US gallons) a week in the case of a dripping tap. If you have a water meter, one way of checking whether or not your system has a leak is to shut off the water and take two meter readings a few minutes apart. If they differ, there is probably a leak.

▶ Install a low-flush toilet. Alternatively, you can reduce the amount of water required to flush the toilet by displacing water in the cistern. The old method was to put a brick in the cistern. Plastic bottles filled with pebbles or water do the same job. There are also similar devices available from water utility companies which can save between 1 and 3 litres (¼ and ¾ US gallons) per flush.

▶ Flow regulators are available which cut the flows from taps (faucets) and shower heads.

▶ During World War II, people in Britain saved water by painting a 'plimsoll' line round the inside of the bathtub as a reminder not to fill it more than a few inches. Shallow baths consume less water than deep ones; showers use even less. The exception is power showers, which can deliver substantial volumes of water in a short space of time.

▶ Running taps send 9 litres (2⅖ US gallons) of clean water down the drain per minute. Try not to leave the tap flowing in full spate while cleaning your teeth. Wash hands in a plugged sink, rather than under a running tap.

▶ Metering your water supply can make you more conscious of how much you are using.

▶ Run full loads in washing machines. Choose appliances that are both water and energy saving – and use those options.

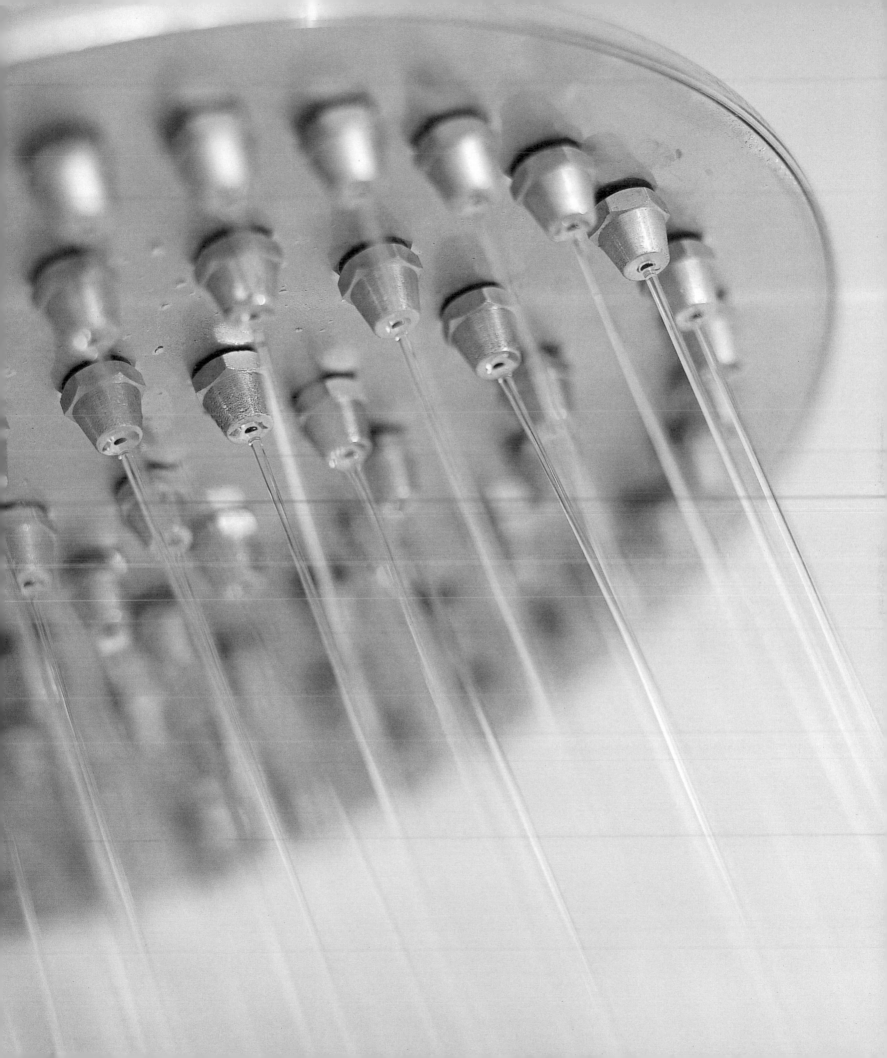

SUPPLIERS

Advice

AMERICAN INSTITUTE OF ARCHITECTS (AIA)
1735 New York Avenue, NW, Washington, DC 20006-5292, USA
Phone: 1-800-AIA-3837
Fax: 202-626-7457
www.aia.org

CARE DESIGN
Moorgate, Ormskirk, Lancashire L39 4RX, UK
Phone: 01695 579061
www.care-design.co.uk
Specialists in bathrooms for the disabled

CERAMIC TILE INSTITUTE OF AMERICA INC. (CTIOA)
12061 Jefferson Boulevard, Culver City, CA 90230-6219, USA
Phone: 310-574-7800
Fax: 310-821-4655
www.ctioa.org

CONSUMER'S ASSOCIATION
2 Marylebone Road, London NWI 4DF, UK
Phone: 020 7770 7000
www.which.net

DISABLED LIVING FOUNDATION
380–384 Harrow Road, London W9 2HU, UK
Phone: 0845 130 9177
www.dlf.org.uk
Information on equipment for the disabled

ELECTRICAL CONTRACTORS' ASSOCIATION
Esca House, 34 Palace Court, London WC2 4HY, UK
Phone: 020 7313 4800
www.eca.co.uk

FEDERATION OF MASTER BUILDERS
Gordon Fisher House, 14–15 Great James Street, London WC1N 3DP, UK
www.fmb.org.uk

INSTITUTE OF PLUMBING
64 Station Lane, Hornchurch, Essex RM12 6NB, UK
Phone: 01708 472791
www.plumbers.org.uk

NATIONAL KITCHEN & BATH ASSOCIATION
687 Willow Grove Street, Hackettstown NJ 07840, USA
Phone: 877-NKBA-PRO
Fax: 908-852-1695
www.nkba.org
Directory of certified bathroom designers and industry guidelines

PLUMBING HEATING COOLING CONTRACTORS NATIONAL ASSOCIATION (PHCC)
180 South Washington Street, PO Box 6808, Falls Church VA 22040, USA
Phone: 703-237-8100
Toll-free: 1-800-533-7694
Fax: 703-237-7442
www.phccweb.org

ROYAL INSTITUTE OF BRITISH ARCHITECTS
66 Portland Place, London W1N 4AD, UK
Phone: 020 7580 5533
www.riba.org

ROYAL INSTITUTE OF CHARTERED SURVEYORS
RICS Contact Centre, Surveyor Court, Westwood Way, Coventry CV4 8SE, UK
Phone: 0870 333 1600
www.rics.org.uk

Fixtures: manufacturers and stockists

AGAPE
via Po Barna, 69,
46031 Correggio Micheli
di Bagnola San Vito,
Milan, Italy
Phone: 0376 250311
Fax: 0376 250330
www.agapedesign.it
Manufacturers of bathroom products and accessories

ALESSI
via Privata Alessi, 6-28882
Crusinallo-Omega, Italy
Phone: 0323 86811
www.alessi.it
for stockits worldwide

ALTERNATIVE PLANS
9 Hester Road, London
SW11 4AN, UK
Phone: 020 7220 6400
www.alternative-plans.co.uk
Bathroom fixtures in stone, timber, glass, stainless steel, ceramic, and acrylic

ARMITAGE SHANKS
Rugeley, Staffordshire
WS15 4BT, UK
Phone: 01543 490253
www.armitage-shanks.co.uk
for suppliers nationwide

ASTON MATTHEWS
141–147a Essex Road,
London N1 2SN, UK
Phone: 020 7226 7220
www.astonmatthews.co.uk

AVANTE BATHROOM PRODUCTS
Thistle House, Thistle Way,
Gildersome Spur, Morley,
Leeds LS27 7JZ, UK
Phone: 0113 201 2240
www.avantebathrooms.com

B & Q
www.diy.com
for stores throughout the UK

BATHAUS
92 Brompton Road,
London SW3 1ER, UK
Phone: 020 7225 7620
Fax: 020 7225 7630
www.bathaus.co.uk

BOFFI
via Oberdan,
70-20030, Lentate sul
Seveso, Milan, Italy
Phone: 0362 5341
Fax: 0362 565077
www.boffi.com
Bathroom manufacturers

CAPITAL MARBLE DESIGN
1 Pall Mall Deposit,
124–128 Barlby Road,
London W10 6BL, UK
Phone: 020 8968 5340
or 020 8960 3131
www.capitalmarble.co.uk
Marble bathroom fixtures

CERAMICA FLAMINIA
SS Flaminia Km. 54,630,
01033 Civita Castellana
(VT), Italy
Phone: 0761 542030
Fax: 0761 540069
www.ceramicaflaminia.it
Manufacturers of sanitaryware

THE CONRAN SHOP
Michelin House, 81 Fulham
Road, London SW3 6RD, UK
Phone: 020 7589 7401
www.conran.co.uk

C P HART & SONS
Newnham Terrace
Hercules Road
London SE1 7DR
Phone: 020 7902 1000
for branches nationwide

CZECH & SPEAKE
39c Jermyn Street,
London SW1 6DN, UK
Phone: 020 7439 0216
Fax: 020 7225 3407
Freephone: 0800 919 728
www.czechspeake.com
Manufacturers of bathroom taps (faucets) and fixtures, including range by David Chipperfield

In the USA:
Toll-free: 1-800-5678-1234

DORNBRACHT
Köbbingser Mühle 6,
D-58640 Iserlohn, Germany
Phone: 02371 433 0
www.dornbracht.com
Manufacturers of sanitaryware

DURAVIT
Werderstrasse 36,
78132 Hornberg,
Germany
Phone: 07833 70 0
Fax: 07833 70 289
www.duravit.com
Manufacturers of sanitaryware by designers such as Starck, Foster, and Sieger Design

DURAVIT USA, INC
1750 Breckinridge Parkway,
Suite 500, Duluth
GA 30096, USA
Phone: 1-770-931-3575
Toll-free: 1-888-387-2848
info@usa.duravit.com

FRANZ KALDEWEI
Beckumer Strasse 33–35,
D-59229 Ahlen, Germany
Phone: 02382 7850
Fax: 02378 5200
www.kaldewei.com
Bathroom manufacturers

HOBSONS CHOICE
Gloucester House County
Park, Shrivenham Road,
Swindon SN1 2NR, UK
Phone: 01793 490685
Fax: 01793 615982
Stockists of Dornbracht products

IDEAL STANDARD
The Bathroom Works,
National Avenue,
Hull HU5 4HS, UK
Phone: 01482 346461
www.ideal-standard.co.uk
for suppliers nationwide

JACUZZI INC
2121 N. California Blvd,
Suite 475, Walnut Creek
CA 94596, USA
Phone: 925-938-7070
www.jacuzzi.com

JACUZZI UK
Silverdale Road,
Newcastle-under-Lyme,
Staffordshire ST5 6EL, UK
Phone: 01782 717175
Fax: 01782 717166
www.jacuzzi.co.uk

JOHN STANLEY
Lagrange, Tamworth,
Staffordshire B79 7XD, UK
Phone: 01827 304000
Fax: 01827 68553
www.johnstanley.com

KOHLER CO.
Kohler, Wisconsin
Phone: 1-800-456-4537
www.kohler.com
Leading American manufacturers of sanitaryware, including spa and whirlpool baths

In the UK:
Phone: 0870 850 5551
www.kohleruk.com

LAUFEN LTD
Laufen House, Crab
Apple Way, Vale Park,
Evesham, Worcestershire
WR11 1GP, UK
Phone: 01386 422768
www.laufen.co.uk or
www.laufen.com
Swiss sanitaryware manufacturers, including a range by Alessi

LEFROY BROOKS
Ibroc House, Essex Road
Hoddesdon, Hertfordshire
EN11 0QS, UK
Phone: 01992 448300
www.lefroybrooks.com
for showrooms nationwide

MAGNET
www.magnet.co.uk
for stores throughout the UK

MAJESTIC SHOWER COMPANY LTD
1 North Place, Edinburgh
Way, Harlow, Essex
CM20 2SL, UK
Phone: 01279 443644
www.majesticshowers.com
for suppliers nationwide
Shower fittings

MFI
www.mfi.co.uk
for stores throughout the UK

ORIGINAL BATHROOMS LTD
143–145 Kew Road,
Richmond, Surrey
TW9 2PN, UK
Phone: 020 8940 7554
Fax: 020 8948 8200

TYLÖ LTD
302 50 Halmstad,
Sweden
Phone: 35 10 00 80
www.tylo.se
Manufacturers of saunas and steam cabins

In the UK:
336–338 Molesey Road,
Hersham, Surrey
KT12 3PD, UK
Phone: 01932 250350
www.tylo.co.uk

VILLEROY & BOCH
Postfach 11 22,
66688 Mettlach,
Germany
Phone: 06864 81 15 00
www.villeroy-boch.com
*Manufacturer of bathroom
products – range designed
by Conran & Partners*

In the UK:
267 Merton Road,
London SW18 5JS, UK
Phone: 020 8871 4028

VOLA UK
Unit 12, Ampthill Business
Park, Station Road,
Ampthill, Bedfordshire
MK45 2QW, UK
Phone: 01525 841155
*Contemporary taps
(faucets)*

WATERWORKS
469 Broome Street,
New York, NY 10013, USA
Phone: 212-966-0605

**WEST ONE BATHROOMS
GROUP LTD**
45–46 South Audley Street,
London W1K 2PY, UK
Phone: 020 7499 1845
Fax: 020 7629 9311
www.westonebathrooms.com

WILLIAM GARVEY
Leyhill, Upton,
Payhembury, Honiton,
Devon EX14 3JG, UK
Phone: 01404 841430
www.williamgarvey.co.uk
Timber baths and sinks

Home furnishings and bathroom products
BED BATH AND BEYOND
Toll-free: 1-800-462-3966
www.bedbathandbeyond.com
for stores throughout
the USA

THE CONRAN SHOP
Michelin House,
81 Fulham Road,
London SW3 6RD, UK
Phone: 020 7589 7401
www.conran.co.uk
and branches worldwide

THE TERENCE CONRAN SHOP
407 East 59th Street,
New York, NY 10022, USA
Toll-free: 1-866-755-9079
www.conran.com

HABITAT
The Heal's Building,
196 Tottenham Court Road,
London W1T 7LD, UK
Phone: 020 7631 3880
www.habitat.net
and branches nationwide

HEAL'S
The Heal's Building,
196 Tottenham Court Road,
London W1T 7LD, UK
Phone: 020 7636 1666
www.heals.co.uk

IKEA
255 North Circular Road,
London NW13 0QJ, UK
Phone: 0845 355 1144
www.ikea.com
and branches nationwide

In the USA:
Toll-free: 1-800-434-4532
Fax: 1-800-329-4532
for stores nationwide

JOHN LEWIS
Oxford Street, London
W1A 1EX, UK
Phone: 08456 049049
www.johnlewis.com
and branches nationwide

POTTERY BARN
Toll-free: 1-888-779-5176
Fax: 702-363-2541
www.potterybarn.com
for stores throughout
the USA

Heating
BISQUE
244 Belsize Road, London
NW6 4BT, UK
Phone: 020 7328 2225
www.bisque.co.uk
Contemporary radiators

MHS RADIATORS
35 Nobel Square,
Burnt Mills Industrial
Estate, Basildon, Essex
SS13 1LT, UK
Phone: 01268 591010
Fax: 01268 728202
www.mhsradiators.com

Lighting
ARTEMIDE
106 Great Russell Street,
London WC1B 3LJ, UK
Phone: 020 7631 5200
www.artemide.com

FLOS INC
200 McKay Road,
Huntingdon Station,
NY 11740, USA
Phone: 516-549-2745
www.flos.net
and suppliers worldwide

LIGHTING UNIVERSE
www.lightinguniverse.com
*Huge range of products and
free shipping service*

**THE LONDON
LIGHTING COMPANY**
135 Fulham Road,
London SW3 6RT, UK
Phone: 020 7589 3612

LUCEPLAN USA
315 Hudson Street,
New York, NY 10013, USA
Phone: 212-691-8263

PROGRESS LIGHTING
www.progresslighting.com
*Information about lighting
applications and on-line
shopping*

VIADUCT
1–10 Summers Street,
London EC1R 5BD, UK
Phone: 020 7278 8456
www.viaduct.co.uk

Surfaces and finishes
Composite
CORIAN
www.corian.com

TONESTER LTD
Huhdantie 4,
21140 Rymättylä,
Finland
Phone: 358 2 252 1000
Fax: 358 2 252 1022
www.durat.com
Manufacturers of Durat

Concrete and plaster
CHRIS TOWNLEY
208 Bowery, New York
NY 10012, USA
Phone: 212-941-1606
Plaster

PAUL DAVIES DESIGN
Unit 5, Parkworks,
16 Park Road,
Kingston-upon-Thames,
KT2 6BG, UK
Phone: 020 8541 0838
*Concrete worktops, baths,
and sinks*

Glass
BENDHEIM GLASS
122 Hudson Street, New
York NY 10013, USA
Phone: 212-226-6370

CESAR COLOR INC
4625 S 32nd Street,
Phoenix, AZ 85040, USA

FUSION GLASS DESIGNS LTD
365 Clapham Road,
London SW9 9BT, UK
Phone: 020 7738 5888

GLASS BLOCKS UNLIMITED
126 East 16th Street, Costa
Mesa CA 92627, USA
Phone: 949-548-8531
Toll-free: 1-800-992-9938
www.glassblocksunlimited.
com

HOURGLASS
Unit 14, The Tanneries,
Brockhampton Lane,
Havant, Hampshire
PO9 1JB, UK
Phone: 023 9248 9900

J PREEDY AND SONS
Lamb Works, North Road,
London N7 9DP, UK
Phone: 020 7700 0377

**PILKINGTON UNITED
KINGDOM LTD**
Prescot Road, St Helens,
Cheshire WA10 3TT, USA
Phone: 01744 692000

SWEDECOR LIMITED
Manchester Street,
Hull HU3 4TX, UK
Phone: 01482 329691

Metal
GOODING ALUMINIUM LTD
1 British Wharf, Landmann
Way, London SE14 5RS, UK
Phone: 020 8692 2255
www.goodingalum.com

Rubber, linoleum, and vinyl

AMTICO
Kingfield Road, Coventry,
Warwickshire CV6 5AA, UK
Phone: 024 7686 1400
Fax: 024 7686 1552
www.amtico.co.uk
Vinyl

DALSOUPLE
PO Box 140,
Bridgwater, Somerset
TA5 1HT, UK
Phone: 0127 872 7777
Fax: 0127 872 7788
www.dalsouple.com
Rubber

DLW LINOLEUM
Armstrong World
Industries, 2500 Columbia
Avenue, PO Box 3001,
Lancaster PA 17604, USA
Phone: 717-397-0611
Toll-free: 1-877-276-7876
www.armstrong.com

FORBO INDUSTRIES, INC
Humboldt Industrial Park,
Maplewood Drive,
PO Box 667, Hazleton
PA 18201, USA
Phone: 570-459-0771
Fax: 570-450-0258
Toll-free: 1-800-842-7839
www.forbo-industries.com
Linoleum

FORBO-NAIRN LTD
PO Box 1, Kirkcaldy,
Fife KY1 2SB, Scotland, UK
Phone: 01592 643 777
Fax: 01592 643 999
www.forbo-nairn.co.uk

**JAYMART RUBBER
& PLASTICS LTD**
Woodlands Trading
Estate, Eden Vale Road,
Westbury, Wiltshire
BA13 3QS, UK
Phone: 01373 864926

Stone

ATTICA
543 Battersea Park Road,
London SW11 3BL, UK
Phone: 020 7738 1234

**CROSSVILLE
PORCELAIN STONE**
PO Box 1168, Crossville
TN 38557, USA
Phone: 931-484-2110
www.crossville-ceramics.com
Stone tile

DELABOLE SLATE
Pengelly, Delabole,
Cornwall PL33 9AZ, UK
Phone: 01840 212242

FORO
140 3rd Street, Brooklyn
NY 11231, USA
Phone: 718-852-2322

KIRKSTONE
128 Walham Green
Court, Moore Park Road,
London SW6 4DG, UK
Phone: 020 7381 0424
www.kirkstone.com

LIMESTONE GALLERY LTD
Arch 47, South
Lambeth Road, London
SW8 1SS, UK
Phone: 020 7735 8555

PARIS CERAMICS
583 Kings Road,
London SW6 9DU, UK
Phone: 020 7371 7778
www.parisceramics.com

In the USA:
150 East 58th Street,
7th Floor, New York,
NY 10155, USA
Phone: 1-212-644-2782
www.parisceramics.com

STONE AGE LTD
19 Filmer Road, London
SW6 7BU, UK
Phone: 020 7385 7954
www.estone.co.uk

STONE PRODUCTIONS LTD
7–9 East Hill, London
SW18 2HYT, UK
Phone: 020 8871 9257

Tile and mosaic

BISAZZA
36041 Alte, Vicenza, Italy
Phone: 0444 707511
Fax: 0444 492088
www.bisazza.it
Manufacturers of mosaic

In the USA:
12 West 23rd Street,
3rd Floor, New York NY
10010, USA
Phone: 212-463-0624
www.bisazza.com

FIRED EARTH
Twyford Mill, Oxford Road,
Adderbury, Oxfordshire
OX17 3HP, UK
Phone: 01295 812088
www.firedearth.com

**THE LIFE ENHANCING
TILE COMPANY**
Unit 3B, Central
Trading Estate,
Bath Road, Bristol
BS4 3EH, UK
Phone: 0117 977 4600

THE MOSAIC WORKSHOP
Unit B, 443–449 Holloway
Road, London N7 6LJ, UK
Phone: 020 7263 2997

**QUILIGOTTI TERRAZZO
TILES LTD**
PO Box 4, Clifton Junction,
Manchester M27 8LP, UK
Phone: 0161 7727 1000
Fax: 0161 727 1122
www.quiligotti.com

RENFROW TILE
1822 Sunnyside
Avenue, Charlotte
NC 28204, USA
Phone: 704-334-6811

WORLD'S END TILES
Silverthorne Road,
London SW8 3HE, UK
Phone: 020 7819 2110
Fax: 020 7819 2101
www.worldsendtiles.co.uk

Wood

DESIGNER WOOD FLOORING
446 W 38th Street, New
York NY 10018, USA
Phone: 212-971-0226

FINEWOOD FLOORS LTD
Suite F4, Skillion
Business Centre, Lea
Valley Trading Estate,
London N18 3BP, UK
Phone: 020 8365 0222

JUNCKERS LTD
Wheaton Court
Commercial Centre,
Wheaton Road, Witham,
Essex CM8 3UJ, UK
Phone: 01376 517512
www.junckers.co.uk

JUNCKERS HARDWOOD INC.
4920 East Landon Drive,
Anaheim, CA 92807, USA
Phone: 714-777-6430
Toll-free: 1 800 878 9663
www.junckershardwood.com

KAHRS (UK) LTD
Unit 2 West, 68 Bognor
Road, Chichester, West
Sussex PO19 2NF, UK
Phone: 01243 778747

KENTUCKY WOOD FLOOR
PO Box 33726, Louisville,
KY 40232, USA
Phone: 800-235-5235

SOLID FLOOR
128 St John Street, London
EC1V 4JS, UK
Phone: 020 7251 2917
www.solidfloor.co.uk

Salvage

AMERICAN SALVAGE
9200 NW 27th Ave, Miami
FL 33147, USA
Phone: 305-836-4444
Fax: 305-691-0001
www.americansalvage.com

**ARCHITECTURAL
SALVAGE REGISTER**
Hutton & Rostron,
Netley House, Gormshall
GU5 9QA, UK
Phone: 01483 203221
Fax: 01483 202911
*Information on architectural
materials suppliers*

**CENTER MILLS
ANTIQUE FLOORS**
PO Box 16, Aspers
PA 17304, USA
Phone: 717-334-0249
Fax: 717-334-6223
*Salvaged wood products,
including flooring*

LASSCO
St Michael's, Mark Street,
London EC2A 4ER, UK
Phone: 020 7749 9944
Fax: 020 7749 9941
www.lassco.co.uk

WALCOT RECLAMATION
108 Walcot Street, Bath
BA1 5BT, UK
Phone: 01225 444404
www.walcot.com

**WHOLE HOUSE
BUILDING SUPPLY**
731-D Loma Verde
Avenue, Palo Alto
CA 94303-4161, USA
Phone: 650-856-0634
Toll-free: 1-800-364-0634
www.driftwoodsalvage.com

INDEX

ACKNOWLEDGMENTS

The publisher would like to thank the following photographers, agencies, and companies for their kind permission to reproduce the following photographs. Every effort has been made to trace the copyright holders. We apologize in advance for any unintentional omissions and would be pleased to insert the appropriate acknowlegment in any subsequent publication.

1 Hotze Eisma/Taverne Agency (Stylist: Hanne Lise Poli); 4 Alexander van Berge/Taverne Agency/Elle Wonen; 5 above Agape/Alternative Plans (www.alternative-plans.co.uk); 5 centre above Geoff Lung; 5 centre below Daniel Farmer/Living Etc/IPC Syndication; 5 below Richard Powers; 7 Paul Massey/Mainstream; 8 Ken Straiton/Corbis; 9 Edmund Sumner/View (Architects: Nicholas Grimshaw & Partners); 10–11 Virginia Del Giudice; 13 Christopher Simon Sykes/World of Interiors (Packwood House, with kind permission from The National Trust); 14 Mirjam Bleeker (Designer: Agnes Emery); 15 Jan Baldwin/Narratives; 16 Heiner Orth; 17 Giulio Oriani/Vega MG; 18 Sue Barr/View; 19 Thomas Popinger/Dornbracht by Sieger Design & Mike Meire; 21 Keith Collie (Architects: Azman Owens); 22 B Miebach/Red Cover; 23 D Brandsma/VT Wonen/Sanoma Syndication (Stylist: Desiree van Dijk); 24 Abode UK; 25 Ferran Freixa/RBA Revistas SA; 26 Verne Fotografie; 26–7 Benny Chan; 28 Sofie Helsted/House of Pictures (Stylist: Lisbett Wedendahl); 29 Richard Powers; 30 A Ianniello/Studiopep; 32 Eugeni Pons/Vega MG; 33 left James Morris/Axiom Photographic Agency; 33 right Verne Fotografie; 34 Agape/Alternative Plans (www.alternative-plans.co.uk); 35 left Inside/Red Cover; 35 right Tim Evan Cook/Red Cover; 36–7 Dennis Gilbert/View (Architect: David Chipperfield); 39 above left Alexander van Berge/Taverne Agency/Rianne Landstra; 39 Alexander van Berge/Taverne Agency/Rianne Landstra; 41 Luke White/The Interior Archive; 42 above Ray Main/Mainstream (De La Cuona); 42 below Ray Main/Mainstream; 43 Chris Tubbs/Red Cover; 44 –5 Giorgio Possenti/Vega MG; 46 Andreas von Einsiedel/Red Cover; 47 Mai-Linh/Marie Claire Maison (Stylist: C Ardouin); 48–9 James Morris/Axiom Photographic Agency (Architect: Claudio Silvestrin); 50 Deidi von Schaewen (Architect: A Putman); 51 above Eduardo Munoz/The Interior Archive (Architect: Nico Rensch); 51 below Bruno Helbling (Architect: Samuel Lerch); 52 Christophe Dugied/Marie Claire Maison (Stylist: Puech/Postic); 53 above Antoine Rozès (Interior Design: Philippe Guilmin); 53 below P Planells/Red Cover; 54 Sorgo Brison (Architect: Joel Caisse); 55 Undine Prohl (Architect: Cigolle/Col); 56–7 Winfried Heinze/Conran Octopus (Architect: Peter Stern; Stylist: Melinda Ashton Turner); 58–9 M Hoyle/Inside; 60 above Alexander van Berge/Taverne Agency/Elle Wonen; 60 below Alexander van Berge/Taverne Agency/VT Wonen; 61 Stellan Herner (Stylist: Synnove Mork); 62 above Hotze Eisma/Taverne Agency (Stylist: Hanne Lise Poli); 62 below Jean Luc Laloux (Interior Design: Instore); 63 Winfried Heinze/Red Cover (Designer: Nibletts); 64 above Verne Fotografie; 64 below Simon Kenny; 65 left Fabio Lombria/Vega MG; 65 right Gianni Basso/Vega MG; 66–9 Lars Ranek/Linnea Press (Stylist: Pernille Vest); 70 above Heidi Grassley/Axiom Photographic Agency (Architect: Seth Stein); 70 below Ray Main/Mainstream; 71 Julie Phipps/View; 72 above Peter Durant/Arcblue (Architect: Alan Phillips); 72 below Paul Massey/Living Etc/IPC Syndication; 73 Stellan Herner (Stylist: Lotta Noremark); 74 Reto Guntli/Red Cover (Designer: Conchita Kien); 75 Richard Powers; 76–7 Giulio Oriani/Vega MG; 78 Ray Main/Mainstream (Design by Filer & Cox), 79 Christian Sarramon; 80 left Ray Main/Mainstream; 80 right Mark Luscombe-Whyte/The Interior Archive (Architect: Anthony Hudson); 81 left Richard Powers; 81 right Jake Curtis/Living Etc/IPC Syndication; 82 Ed Reeve/Red Cover; 83 left Eugeni Pons/Vega MG; 83 right Richard Powers; 84 Edmund Sumner/View; 85 left Mark Luscombe-Whyte/Homes & Gardens/IPC Syndication; 85 right Jake Fitzjones/Living Etc/IPC Syndication; 86–7 Henry Wilson/Red Cover (Architect: Ian Chee); 88 Richard Powers; 89 Verne Fotografie; 90 left E Morin/Marie Claire Maison (Stylist: C Ardouin); 90 right Peter Dixon/Narratives; 91 Geoff Lung Architect: Andrew Nolan; Owner: Rory O'Brien); 92 Richard Bryant/Arcaid (Architect: Seth Stein); 93 Undine Prohl (Architect: Rick Joy); 94 left Erck Saillet/Red Cover; 94 right Peter Cook/View (Architect: Bluebase); 95 Hotze Eisma/Taverne Agency (Stylist: Hanne Lise Poli); 96 Hotze Eisman/Taverne Agency (Architect: Wim de Vos; Stylist: Marielle Maesssen); 97 left Hotze Eisman/Taverne Agency (Architect: Wim de Vos; Stylist: Marielle Maesssen); 97 right Hotze Eisman/Taverne Agency (Architect: Wim de Vos; Stylist: Rianne Landstra); 98 above Paul Massey/living Etc/IPC Syndication; 98 below Tom Scott/View (Architect: Forster Inc); 99 Tom Scott/View (Architect: Forster Inc); 100 Mark Luscombe-Whyte/The Interior Archive (Architect: Anthony Hudson), 101 Richard Bryant/Arcaid (Architect: Bushe Associates); 102 Verne Fotografie; 102–3 Alexander Van Berge/Taverne Agency/Elle Wonen; 104–5 Eugeni Pons/Vega MG; 106 left Richard Powers; 106 right Dexter Hodges/Lovatt Smith Interiors; 107 Mai-Linh/Marie Claire Maison (Stylist: C Ardouin); 108–9 E Huibers/Sanoma Syndication; 109 Ray Main/Mainstream (Architect: Patel Taylor Architects); 110 left Andreas von Einsiedel (Designer: Charles Style); 110 right Ray Main/Mainstream (Architect: Gregory Phillips); 111 Kohler courtesy of Hill & Knowlton; 112 Geoff Lung/Arcaid (Architect: Luigi Rosselli); 113 left Jasper James/Elle Decoration (Stylists: Bowles & Linares; Homeowner: Skin); 113 right Richard Powers; 114 F Vasseur/Red Cover; 115 Bruno Helbling (Architect: Samuel Lerch); 116–17 Paul Ryan/International Interiors (Architect: Kastrup-Sjunneson); 118 Nick Guttridge/View (Architect: Julian Arendt); 119 James Morris/Axiom Photographic Agency (Architect: Georg Driendl); 120 above Jean Luc Laloux (Architect: S Godsell); 120 below Geoff Lung (Architect: Iain Halliday; Owner: Sarah Cottier and Ashley Barbour); 121 James Morris/Axiom Photographic Agency (Architect: George Driendl); 122 Jean Luc Laloux (Architect: S Godsell); 122–3 Undine Prohl (Architect: LMS); 123 Undine Prohl (Architect: A Kalach); 124 above Karin Bjorkquist (Stylist: Gill Renlund); 124 below Geoff Lung (Architect: Robert Riddell; Owner: Pam Easton and Robert Riddell); 125 Richard Powers; 126 Andrea Ferrari; 127 above Michael Moran (Interior Designers: Tod Williams Billie Tsien); 127 below Verne Fotografie; 128–31 Winfried Heinze/Conran Octopus (Architects: Zombory-Moldovan Moore; Stylist: Melinda Ashton Turner); 132–3 James Morris/Axiom Photographic Agency; 134 Grazia Ike Branco; 135 Stellan Herner (Stylist: Lotta Noremark); 136 Bieke Claessens; 137 above Mark Luscombe-Whyte/The Interior Archive (Designer: Gune Wardena); 137 below Verity Welstead/Red Cover (Designer: Fred Collins); 138 Paul Ryan/International Interiors (Architect: Kastrup-Sjunnesson); 139 left Bieke Claessens (Interior Design: Cy Peys); 139 right Agape/Alternative Plans (www.alternative-plans.co.uk); 140 above Sharyn Cairns (Architect: Jaci Foti-Lowe); 140 below West One Bathrooms; 141 Minh & Wass (Designer: Tyler Hays for BDDW); 142 Minh & Wass (Designer: David Khouri); 143 left James Morris/Axiom Photographic Agency, 143 right Minh & Wass; 144 above Alexander van Berge/Taverne Agency/Reini Smit; 144 below James Morris/Axiom Photographic Agency (Architect: Claudio Silvestrin); 145 Hotze Eisma/Taverne Agency (Stylist: Rianne Landstra); 146 left Simon Whitmore/Living Etc/IPC Syndication; 146 right Helen Pe/House of Pictures (Stylist: Roth & Stone Production, Designer: Claes v Hauswolff); 147 left Chris Tubbs/Red Cover; 147 right Minh & Wass; 149 Nick Hufton/View; 150 left Bieke Claessens; 150 right Simon Whitmore/Living Etc/IPC Syndication; 151 Verne Fotografie; 152 Bieke Claessens (Interior Designer: Simon Chottovelli); 152–3 Original Bathrooms Ltd; ; 154 left Mai-Linh/Marie Claire Maison (Stylist: C Ardouin); 154 right H del Olmo/Inside/Red Cover; 155 Richard Powers; 156 left Richard Glover/View (Architect: Form Design & Architecture); 156 right Nicholas Tosi/Marie Claire Maison (Stylists: Ardonin/Bayle/Reyre); 157 Gianni Basso/Vega MG, 158 left Daniel Farmer/Living Etc/IPC Syndication; 158 right Sigurd Kranendonk/Dornbracht; 159 left Richard Powers; 159 right Thomas Popinger/Dornbracht by Sieger Design & Mike Meire; 160 left Hotze Eisma/Taverne Agency (Stylist: Rianne Landstra);160 right Thomas Popinger/Dornbracht by Sieger Design & Mike Meire;161 Camera Press/Visi/Ryno (Architect: Arthur Quinton); 162 above left Luc Wauman; 162 above right Ray Main/Mainstream; 162 below left Guy Obijn; 162 below right Jefferson Smith/Arcblue (Architect: Dive Architects), 164 Grazia Ike Branco; 165 above Chris Gascoigne/View (Architect: John Kerr Associates); 165 below Richard Glover/View (Interior Designer: Ivan Bussens); 166 Eugeni Pons/Vega MG; 167 V T'Sas/Red Cover; 168 left Jefferson Smith/Arcblue (Interior Design: Dive Architects); 168 right Nick Hufton/View(Architect: Wells Mackereth); 169 left Dennis Gilbert/View (Architect: Brady Mallalieu); 169 right Philip Sowells/Digital Home Magazine; 170 left Chris Tubbs; 170 right Andreas von Einsiedel (Designer: Jane McCormack); 171 left MHS radiators (www.mhsradiators.com); 171 right James Balston/Arcblue (Interior Design: ZYNK Design consultants); 172 Tom Scott/Living Etc/IPC Syndication; 173 Christopher Drake/Red Cover (Interior Design: Catherine Memmi); 174 left Jake Fitzjones/Red Cover (Designer: Debbie Hatchwell); 174 right Giulio Oriani/Vega MG; 175 above Jean Luc Laloux (Architect: Vincent Van Duysen); 175 below Alexander van Berge/Taverne Agency/Reini Smit; 176 Ray Main/Mainstream (Architects: AKK Architects); 177 Ray Main/Mainstream (Designers: Collett-Zarzycki); 178 Andrew Twort/Red Cover (Designer: Osborne & Little); 179 above left Bruno Helbling; 179 above right Richard Powers; 179 below Julie Phipps/View (Architect: Tim Lawrence); 181 Cristina Rodés/Lovatt Smith Interiors; 183 Alun Callender; 184 Tom Scott/Living Etc/IPC Syndication; 185 left Alexander van Berge/Taverne Agency/Ulrika Lundgren; 185 right Dennis Gilbert/View (Architects: James Melvin & Gollins Melvin Ward & partners); 186 Jean Luc Laloux (Architects: Legorreta & Legorreta); 187 above Bruno Helbling; 187 below Giorgio Possenti/Vega MG; 188 left Minh & Wass (Designer: Karim Rashid); 188 right Minh & Wass; 189 Paul Massey/Mainstream; 190 above Jan Baldwin/Narratives; 190 below Undine Prohl (Architect: A Kalach); 191 Alexander van Berge/Taverne Agency/Rianne Landstra; 192 left Brian Harrison/Red Cover; 192 right Antoine Rozès (Interior Design: Philippe Guilmin); 193 Ray Main/Mainstream; 195 above Giulio Oriani/Vega MG; 195 below Christoph Kicherer (Architect: Ramon Esteves; Owner: Jose Gandia-Blasco (Ibiza));196 Ray Main/Mainstream (Architect: David Wolf); 197 A Ianniello/Studiopep; 198 left Andreas von Einsiedel (Designer: Abby Yozell); 198 right Hotze Eisma/Taverne Agency; 199 James Morris/Axiom Photographic Agency; 200 Ray Main/Mainstream (Architects: MMR Architects); 201 left Jefferson Smith/Arcblue (Interior Design: Eric Gizard); 201 right Jean Luc Laloux (Architect: B Gomez Tenarquitectos); 202 above Dennis Gilbert/View; 202 below Verne Fotografie; 203 Jean Luc Laloux (Architects: Legorreta & Legorreta); 204 above left Agape/Alternative Plans (www.alternative-plans.co.uk); 204 above right Winfried Heinze/Red Cover; 204 below Andrew Twort/Red Cover; 205 Giulio Oriani/Vega MG; 206 Graham Atkins-Hughes/Red Cover; 207 Catherine Gratwicke; 209 Ray Main/Mainstream (Property: Chateau De Massillan); 211 Ray Main/Mainstream; 212 Alexander van Berge/Taverne Agency/Rianne Landstra; 214 Mark Williams/Homes & Gardens/IPC Syndication; 215 Ray Main/Mainstream (Developer: Candy & Candy); 216 and 224 Richard Powers

The publishers would like to thank Laurence Pidgeon and Teri Pengelly at Alternative Plans.

_ Would it be ok to stop the Vraylar?

_

+ How long for the effects of the Qua   for the depression?